TRAVELLERS' TRAILS • SCOTLAND

This edition first published in 2001 by
Passport Books, an imprint of the
McGraw-Hill Companies

ISBN:0-658-01544-3

Library of Congress Catalog Card Number: 2001131172

Travellers' Trails • Scotland

David Ross

PASSPORT BOOKS
NTC/Contemporary Publishing Group

Contents

Introduction

In your hands you have a guide book that has been written to help you go deeper than most other guides go – to get under the skin of Scotland. Its range of varied and interlinking trails takes you across the country, into its history and culture, exploring and revealing a distinctive way of life that has evolved in Scotland over many centuries.

How to Use this Book

Divided into about twenty different trails of varying length, *Travellers' Trails: Scotland* takes you on an exploration of Scotland, past and present. It follows themes of interest, and brings a special focus to individual sites and communities. It is not a hotel or restaurant guide, and should be used in conjunction with these. Use it by selecting the trail or trails you would like to follow. Very often, the places you visit will feature in other trails as well. Their names are given in bold type, like this: **Stirling**. If you look up Stirling in the index, you will be able to locate other points of interest there. Each trail is given a length, both in mileages between points and in days (or part-days).

Whilst the longer trails are planned with the car driver in mind, it is worth remembering that Scotland is good cycling country, and that very often cycles may be hired in local centres for a more intimate exploration of the countryside than can be managed in a car. There are also many places only attainable by walking – usually quite a short walk from a car park – and these are clearly indicated. Route instructions have been made as detailed as possible, and are based on the most up-to-date information, but as all drivers know, alterations and local diversions can sometimes be found. A good road atlas (minimum 4 miles to an inch) will be a useful help.

While each trail follows a particular theme, you will find that most of the places you pass through have other associations as well. After all, Scotland has been inhabited for at least 7,000 years and many generations have left their marks (Orkney and the Viking Trail are a good example).

The trails have also been chosen to link up with one another, so that if you find yourself in, say, Inverness, you can "dip into" a choice of other trails – take part of a day to check out the Loch Ness Monster, for instance; or do a section of the Malt Whisky Trail. In Ayrshire, you can follow both William Wallace and Robert Burns.

There are three main starting points for the trails, Edinburgh and Glasgow for the south and the southern Highlands, and Inverness for the north.

THE BASIC BACKGROUND

One of the earliest European countries to achieve nationhood, Scotland has been a single kingdom since 1032. Its final boundaries were not achieved until 1472, however, when Orkney and Shetland, held by Norway since the 9th century, were brought under Scottish rule. In the 11th century, the language of most of the country was Gaelic, but the use of a form of English, called Scots, spread steadily from the south-east. By the end of the 19th century there were only a few hundred people who spoke nothing but Gaelic.

The King of Scotland inherited the Crown of England from his cousin, Elizabeth I of England, when she died in 1603. From then on, Scotland's kings and queens lived in London. Scotland at that time remained a separate nation with its own Parliament. Then in 1707 Scotland united with England and Wales as the United Kingdom of Great Britain, with a single Parliament in London. Scotland retained its national Church, its separate legal and educational systems, and its own local administrative organisations. In 1999 a new Scottish Parliament was set up in Edinburgh. This Parliament has a wide range of internal autonomy but very little in the way of revenue-raising powers. Scotland continues to send representatives to the UK Parliament, and also to the European Parliament. For those interested in finding out more about Scotland's history, see the Recommended Reading at the end of this book.

MODERN SCOTLAND

Scotland is home to some five million people, the great majority of whom live in the "central belt" between Glasgow and Edinburgh. Outside this area there is a vast extent of open countryside. Although the Highland region is one of Europe's great "wilderness" areas, much of the countryside is good farming land, where you will see sheep and cattle in large numbers, often from breeds developed in Scotland, such as the Blackface sheep and Ayrshire or Aberdeen-Angus cattle. It is a countryside of stone-built villages and small towns, often with an 18th- or early 19th-century aspect to their buildings.

As a nation with a large and much more populous neighbour, the Scots have always had to work hard to preserve their own sense of identity. As a result, a variety of distinctive traditions have been maintained here. Best-known are the bagpipe music and the kilt. But it runs far deeper, and one of the pleasures of visiting Scotland is in discovering the ways in which its people are different, in their speech, their eating habits, and their ways of passing the time.

If you have time to spare on your travels in the country, it can be rewarding to look at notices advertising local events. Usually these are not aimed at the "tourist trade", though visitors are welcome. They include such happenings as the "Highland Games", with a wide variety of field sports, for example, tossing the caber. There are sheepdog trials, local carnivals, country dance shows, concerts of folk and traditional music in pubs and halls, and much more. Local events go on through the summer months. You may happen on Selkirk or Hawick at the time of the Common Riding, a rich mixture of pagan tradition and local pride, or come upon a remote Highland spot like Glenfinnan while the Highland Gathering is on.

Scotland and Tourism

Tourism is one of Scotland's major industries, along with farming, whisky and electronics. As a visitor, you are yourself part of a "harvest" helping to sustain the country. This guide book is intended to get you away from the most visitor-haunted places, and to see even these with a focused eye that goes beyond the superficial tartanry. The country has many "heritage centres". These centres, often highly informative, are as much for the benefit of locals as for visitors. They are an aspect of a country coming to terms with rapid change. Forty years ago, you could watch herring boats unload their catch at any of a score of harbours, or get a permit to go down a real working coal mine, or experience the sooty pleasure of a steam train as a matter of course. Today these are "heritage experiences" on offer at museum sites, and inevitably somewhat sanitised in the process. You are looking at "this is how we were", not at "this is how we are". This is of course a worldwide state of affairs. Modern Scotland, like most other countries, stands on top of many layers of history and human experience, and it is always fascinating to dig down through these and get a sense of how the modern scene has been put together.

Entry Times and Admission Charges

Please bear in mind that most of the visitor sites listed have a "last admissions" policy, with no more admissions half an hour before the noted closing time (45 minutes in the case of some). With some exceptions, most "visitor sites" charge for admission to special displays, museums, etc. Again with exceptions, free entry may mean a shop, or an emphasis on retail rather than on information. Tourist Information Centres are always the best places to get free and reliable information on local sites and accommodation. Entry times given in this guide are current at the time of going to press, but are always subject to change.

Driving in Scotland

The rules of the road are the same as for the rest of the United Kingdom. In hilly areas, roads often have tight bends and blind summits, and care is needed when overtaking. There are no long mountain climbs of the Alpine sort – the highest motor road in the country reaches just over 2,000 feet. In Highland areas, sheep often roam across wide stretches of moorland and drivers have to watch out for them on unfenced roads, especially in the dark. There are still some "single-track" roads, where passing places have to be used to allow vehicles to pass one another and also to overtake, though some drivers seem unaware of this. On some of the more far-flung trails, petrol stations may be widely spaced, and it is a good idea to keep your fuel tank topped up. Outside city centres, parking is usually easy and often free.

PUBLIC TRANSPORT IN SCOTLAND

Most of the places in *Travellers' Trails: Scotland* can be reached by public transport. Scotland has a rail network serving major towns, and the rail routes are often highly scenic, especially Edinburgh–Dundee–Aberdeen and Glasgow–Fort William–Mallaig. On the long peripheral lines, like Inverness–Wick or Glasgow–Stranraer, services may consist only of two or three trains a day, so it is important to check timetables or dial the relevant enquiry line. Coach services also link the larger towns and the ferry-ports. In some Highland districts post-bus services operate. Public transport on Sundays is usually much reduced outside the cities and large towns. Scotland also has a good air network, linking Edinburgh, Glasgow and Inverness (the three starting points for the trails) with other airports in Scotland and the international network. These airports also have full car-hire facilities.

WEATHER IN SCOTLAND

For a relatively small country, Scotland has a very changeable weather pattern created by its mountainous terrain and closeness to the sea. It is a northerly country – Edinburgh is at latitude 56 degrees, the same as Moscow and Hudson Bay – and even in summer it can be quite cool at times. As some of the trails take you along footpaths and hill-tracks, you should have good walking shoes and bring weatherproof clothing. It is one of the charms of Scotland that you may need your sun-block and your raincoat on the same day.

Trail 1

The Malt Whisky Story

Two days from Inverness, investigating the mystique of Highland Malt in its heartland

Like all the others, this trail can easily be lengthened to three or more days, simply by taking your time and perhaps exploring some of the many attractions unconnected with the whisky industry. These range from river- and loch-fishing to sightseeing in several baronial castles. Distillery tours normally involve a charge, but this usually includes a free "dram" at the end, and in the case of Strathisla, coffee and shortbread biscuits. It is a good idea to telephone ahead to check the availability of tours, and even how busy the place is. You may not want to share your experience with a coach party of fifty others. As with most places, last admissions are usually half an hour before closing time.

The oldest reference to whisky is found in Scottish government records of 1494. The making of whisky was licensed by the king, and the first distillers were the monks of Scotland's many pre-Reformation (1560) abbeys and priories. The origins of whisky-making go much further back than that. Whisky is an English form of the Gaelic word "uisge", meaning water; and the full name of the drink is "uisge beatha" (pronounced "ooshkavaw") which means "water of life". In the 16th century in Edinburgh and other larger towns, whisky-making became a monopoly of the barber-surgeons, who presumably dosed their patients on it before performing

Glenlivet Distillery, Moray

the somewhat primitive operations of early surgery. Whisky distilling was a small-scale activity. The Scots drank far more ale and, when they could afford it, imported French wine. But after the Reformation, when all monasteries were closed down, the secret rituals of distilling became more public.

The first large-scale distillery was at Ferintosh, just on the outskirts of Dingwall in Ross-shire (Highlands) where there are still old whisky warehouses. This place flourished in the 17th century. But by then many farmers and dwellers in isolated communities were making their own supplies. The great period of illicit whisky-making was the 18th century, when there were many legendary encounters between the whisky-makers and the government's revenue men. One of the most famous whisky-runners was Mansie Eunson, still famous in the Orkney capital of **Kirkwall**.

But by 1823 a government revenue act enabled the modern whisky industry to begin, and it is from this period that the familiar grey stone buildings with their pagoda-like towers (creating air draughts for drying the barley) began to be built in far-off glens and on coastal bays. Helped by the many Scottish settlers in the New World and the Antipodes, whisky became a world drink.

At first blended whisky was the norm, but as the industry has matured – and got more clever at marketing – "single malt" whiskies have become the most talked-about and prized products of the industry. These are the product of a single distillery, unmixed with that of any other, and produced from malted barley. This is harvested barley which has been allowed to start to sprout, or germinate; it is then dried, milled, mixed with water, fermented and distilled. Blended whisky usually includes grain whisky as well, and may be the product of several distilleries. Blending is itself an art and there are many fine blends, but real connoisseurship is linked to the malts. The Highlands are Scotland's prime whisky-producing area and there are five distinctive districts: Speyside, the Northern Highlands, Aberdeenshire, The West Highlands and Inner Hebrides, and **Islay**. This trail focuses on Speyside.

Speyside runs a whisky festival every year at the beginning of May, with many special events, but there is always plenty to see between April and October.

Starting from Inverness, follow the A9 road south (signed for Perth) up into the hills. There is a fine view back across the Beauly Firth from the information centre at Bogbain (5 miles). The road reaches a 1,000ft/360m summit in the narrow Slochd pass; a mile beyond it, turn left on to the A938, signed to Grantown. At Dulnain Bridge you reach the valley of the Spey, said to be the swiftest flowing of the country's main rivers, and also a fine salmon stream. Turn left on to the A95 for Grantown (33 miles from Inverness). You are in the country of Clan Grant here, as the name of Grantown tells. The little town is a pleasant tourist centre largely built from local stone. Grant is not a Gaelic name: it is the same word as the French grand, "big, tall"; the Norman-French Grants established themselves among the Celts here in the 13th century and gradually became thoroughly celtified themselves.

From Grantown take the A95, signed to Craigellachie. Travelling through very picturesque countryside of farmland and rolling hills, you get a sense of how the two main ingredients of whisky are readily available here – barley and good running water. Above the farmland there are moors – at Cromdale in 1690 a battle was fought between supporters of the exiled King James II and those of the recently enthroned King William and Queen Mary. As you drive towards Aberlour, the bulky mountain of Ben Rinnes rises on the right-hand side ahead of you; streams flow off it to north, south and west, all feeding distilleries. On the left-hand side you see Tormore (10 miles), a distillery with an unusual adjunct, a fine woodland garden with specially trimmed hedges and bushes for those who enjoy the fun of topiary. Just under 2 miles on, turn off to the right just past Bridge of Avon (pronounced "A'an" – this is one of the many river names which simply means "water") and the B9008 road will take you to the finely sited Glenlivet Distillery (6 miles) and its visitor centre, with shaggy, long-horned Highland cows grazing outside. Glenlivet also offers its own leaflets on local car and walking tours. If you have time, it is well worth exploring one of these paths. They show how much this apparently wild landscape has been used and adapted by humans, including some primitive whisky-making sites. It was in this glen, on 14 October 1594, that an army led by the Earl of Argyll, fighting on behalf of King James

VI, was defeated by the rebellious Earl of Huntly in a fierce battle in which many old clan scores were also paid off.

Glenlivet Distillery, *Glenlivet, Moray; tel 01542 783220* (open mid March–Oct, Mon–Sat 10am–4pm, Sun 12.30pm–4pm; open to 6pm July–Aug).

For a touch of motoring adventure, you can continue on past Tomnavoulin Distillery ("Hill of the Mill"; the old mill is still preserved) to Tomintoul (11 miles), one of the highest villages in Scotland, with fine vistas south to the Cairngorm Mountains. Here too there is a distillery. The name of Glenlivet is so potent in malt whisky drinking circles that several distilleries have annexed it, including Tomintoul. The actual Glenlivet Distillery, founded in 1824, distinguishes its product by calling it The Glenlivet. From Tomintoul take the northbound A939, turning right after about two miles on to the B9136 road down Strathavon (10 miles); turn left by Glenlivet Distillery on the B9008 heading northwards again to Bridge of Avon (6 miles). These well-surfaced but winding mountain roads are often closed by snow in winter. Turning right on to the A95, you soon reach Glenfarclas Distillery (2 miles), which runs a very good guided tour, and also has an unusual feature in its "Ship's Room", with panelling from the old liner *Empress of Australia*. The stills here are the largest in the region (you will find that much of the mystique of malt whisky resides in the size and shape of each distillery's set of stills). Only 2 miles away across the Spey (turn left on the B9138 at Marypark, then right on to the B9102) is Knockando Distillery (the name means "Hill of the Market"), where part of its "visitor experience" is to show a range of 128 different malt whiskies.

Glenfarclas Distillery, *Ballindalloch, Moray; tel 01807 500245* (open April–Sept, Mon–Fri 9.30am–5pm; Oct–March, Mon–Fri 10am–4pm; June–Sept, Sat 9.30–4.30).

Knockando Distillery, *Knockando, Moray; tel 01340 810205* (open by appointment only).

You are now nearing the heart of the Speyside whisky region. There are "Whisky Trail" road signs put up by the AA (Automobile Association). Be warned though, whisky is pow-

erful stuff and too many free samples have been known to take
drivers a long way – all the way to the sheriff's court in the
county capital of Elgin. Also at Knockando on the B9102 is
Cardhu Distillery (Visitor Centre). Return from here to
Marypark and turn left on to the A95 for Charlestown of
Aberlour (8 miles). Aberlour Distillery, whose water comes
from an old "holy well" dedicated to the Pictish St Drostan, is
not usually open to visitors, though they put on an occasional
"Aberlour Experience".

Cardhu Distillery, *Knockando, Moray; tel 01340 872555*
(open March–Nov, Mon–Fri 9.30am–4.30pm; July–Aug, also
Sat 9.30am–4.30pm, Sun 11am–4pm; Dec–Feb, Mon–Fri
10am–4pm).

Aberlour Distillery, *Charleston of Aberlour, Moray; tel 01340
871204.*

Whisky casks, Speyside
Cooperage, Craigellachie,
Moray

Aberlour village once was home to a large orphanage run by the Episcopal Church in Scotland – a reminder that Scotland is by no means a uniformly Calvinist-Presbyterian society. In this area especially, adherence to the Episcopal Church, and to the pre-Reformation Catholic Church, has always been present. High up on the Braes of Glenlivet – take the little road from Knockandhu on the B9008 and look for Chapeltown signs (about 4 miles each way) – was a secret training school for priests, now restored, at Scalan. Three hundred years ago, this was a remote and hard-to-reach district which took little notice of laws and decisions made in far-off Edinburgh.

Northwards on the A95 lies Craigellachie (2 miles), a junction of routes where Glen Fiddich joins Strathspey. Once a railway junction, its trains have long gone; but there is an engineering feature here, one of the world's first iron bridges (1815), its wrought-iron lattice crossing the Spey in a single 150-foot span. It also has the Speyside Cooperage, where whisky casks are made and maintained (Visitor Centre). Casks are very important in the maturing process; distillers comb the wine-producing countries nowadays for used casks which impart a hint of colour and flavour – sherry used to be the most common, but Madeira-style wine casks are also used today – all part of the trend towards "designer" whiskies which, it is hoped, will keep the industry flourishing.

Speyside Cooperage, *Craigellachie, Moray; tel 01340 871108* (open early Jan–mid Dec, Mon–Fri 9.30am–4.30pm; June–Sept, Sat 9.30am–4pm).

Turn sharply right at Craigellachie on A941 for Dufftown (4 miles), the whisky capital of the region. Its name shows you have passed into the territory of another great clan, the Duffs and Macduffs (the name is Gaelic and means "Dark-haired"), and if you have read or seen Shakespeare's "Macbeth", a reminder that the true scenes from which that tragedy was taken were acted out not far from here. At Dufftown are the Balvenie and Glenfiddich Distilleries. Balvenie preserves the old-style malting floor where the malting barley is turned over by hand. Access to both distilleries is via the Glenfiddich Visitor Centre, a sophisticated one with a multimedia presentation of whisky production.

Glenfiddich Distillery, *Dufftown, Moray; tel 01340 820373* (open early Jan–mid Dec, Mon–Fri 9.30am–4.30pm; Easter–mid Oct, Sat 9.30am–4.30pm; Sun 12 noon–6.30pm).

Dufftown also has a museum (ex-jailhouse) full of local-interest exhibits; the township itself dates from 1817 and is one of many model settlements of that time, replacing the chaotic old farming villages (Grantown and Tomintoul have the same origins and the same "planned" feel). "Heritage" walking tours of Dufftown are usually available. Its gallows site is a reminder of the days – up to 1748 – when the local laird dispensed the king's justice and kept a gallows to hang male malefactors and a pit in which to drown women criminals (in fact capital punishment was rare).

Dufftown Museum, *The Square, Dufftown, Moray; tel 01340 820501* (open April–Oct, Mon–Sat 10am–5pm).

Close to Dufftown there is also a reminder that we are in what was originally Pictish country (see Land of the Picts Trail): the old church at Mortlach (1 mile) has a Pictish carved stone cross in its churchyard. The church building, of the 12th century but very much restored, still has a "lepers' squint" inside: a slanted hole in the wall through which sufferers from leprosy could watch the service.

Each distillery is keen to promote the virtues of its own brand, but if you can participate in a tasting or a "nosing" – the sharpest judges use nose rather than palate – it is intriguing to see how different the whiskies from distilleries that are almost cheek-by-jowl can be. The malt connoisseur not only has to tell his "Speyside" from any other region, but differentiate between the numerous fine Speyside whiskies, which include the Macallan as well as the Glenlivet. You may be intrigued by the complex product that results from the relatively simple distilling process and its combination of ancient processes and modern technology, and perhaps amused by some of the "heritage" information that will be earnestly offered to you. The whisky industry shows modern Scotland very much in action: much thought and ingenuity is going into how to promote it as a 21st-century drink. The discerning visitor can see this process in action too, as the masters of whisky both compete with one another and combine in the struggle to position their product in a fickle world market where many alternatives are on offer.

Turning back from Dufftown to Craigellachie (4 miles), you head north again on the A941, following the Spey valley to Rothes (3 miles), home of the Glen Grant Distillery. As well as touring the distillery, you can walk through the Victorian woodland garden created by Major Grant and now restored.

Glen Grant Distillery & Garden, *Rothes, Moray; tel 01542 783318* (open mid March–Oct, Mon–Sat 10am–4pm, Sun 11.30am–4pm; June–Sept, closes 5pm daily).

From Rothes you leave the Spey valley, driving on the A941 up the pleasant Glen of Rothes, still passing the occasional distillery, towards **Elgin** (10 miles), county town of the old county of Moray and an important whisky centre in its own right. Its prime monument is, however, its ruined cathedral, a fine Gothic structure burned down in 1390 by a bandit known as the "Wolf of Badenoch", who also happened to be son of the reigning king, Robert III, and the man supposedly in charge of administering justice to the whole North of Scotland. Elgin has a very good museum.

Elgin Museum, *1 High St, Elgin, Moray; tel 01343 543675* (open Easter–Oct, Mon–Fri 10am–5pm, Sat 11am–4pm, Sun 2pm–5pm).

If time allows, from Elgin, with its Georgian buildings and stately atmosphere, you can go eastwards to Keith, where there is Scotland's oldest working distillery, Strathisla, founded in 1786. Though malts are our theme, Stathisla will also show you how whisky blending is done. Take the A96 towards Aberdeen; Keith, whose name probably means "wood", is 17 miles (or branch right after 2 miles and follow the B9103 past attractive woodlands into the Spey Valley, cross the river at the former ferry-site at Boat o' Brig, turn left at Mulben on to the A95, and enter Keith from the west). Both roads pass through the "model village" of Fife Keith before the town proper. The distillery is well marked.

Strathisla Distillery, *Seafield Avenue, Keith*; tel 01542 783044 (open Feb–mid March, Mon–Fri 9.30am–4pm; mid March–Nov, Mon–Sat 9.30am–4pm, Sun 12.30pm–4pm).

From Elgin the Whisky Trail returns westwards to Inverness, along the A96. At Forres, there is the museum-distillery of Dallas Dhu, with its informative audio-visual programme. Take the A96 west for 12 miles, at Forres turn left on the A940 towards Grantown, branching left again on the minor road from Knockomie about a mile south of the town, then look out for Dallas Dhu Historic Distillery on the left-hand side.

Dallas Dhu Historic Distillery, *Mannachie Road, Forres, Moray*; tel 01309 676548 (open April–Sept, Mon–Sun 9.30am–6.30pm; Oct–March, Mon–Wed, also Sat 9.30am–4.30pm, Thurs 9.30am–12.30pm, Sun 2pm–4.30pm)

From here, return to the A96. Inverness is 26 miles away, via the beach-resort town of Nairn. At the end of the Whisky Trail, you are near the following trails: Bonnie Prince Charlie, Sutherland Clearances.

TRAIL 2

The Land of Wallace

Two days from Glasgow, exploring the terrain and places associated with the Guardian of Scotland

The film *Braveheart* has spread the story of Sir William Wallace around the world. Whilst its details are open to question (but when did any film provide a completely accurate record of events?) it has ensured that many people know the essential details of the Wallace story. Here is a resumé of Wallace's life.

Born around 1270, he was a young man in the years after 1290 when, the royal family having died out, Scotland was without a king. At that time King Edward I of England presided over the election of the nobleman John Balliol as King of Scotland – but with Edward as his overlord. This proved unworkable: in 1296 there was a short war and Edward forcibly deposed Balliol. Edward's aim to then impose direct rule on Scotland was opposed by guerrilla-type warfare, organised mainly by William Wallace and Andrew Moray. This swiftly grew into a national movement and in 1297 an English army was defeated at Stirling Bridge by Wallace and Moray. Wallace was named as Guardian of Scotland. In the following year Wallace was defeated at Falkirk. Sporadic fighting continued, but in the face of overwhelming opposition, Wallace was virtually the only remaining leader of an anti-English band by 1304. In 1305 he was captured by treachery, taken to London, tried for treason, and barbarically executed.

Wallace crossed Scotland so many times that to follow his travels in chronological order would take many days. Many places feature at different stages of his career and we will put the pieces together as we go.

Glasgow is the starting point. The Glasgow of Wallace's day was a little cathedral city among green fields, a market-place where Highlands and Lowlands met. The choir and crypt of the present cathedral were still new in Wallace's time. Nothing else remains from the period, though the names and layout of streets just south of the cathedral – High Street, Saltmarket, Gallowgate, Trongate, intersecting at Glasgow

Cross – show the original town around which a great city grew in the 18th and 19th centuries.

In 1296 Wallace, with a small band of men, is believed to have driven the English garrison from Glasgow Castle (no remains, though Castle Street retains the name). Near here, at the junction of High Street and Bell Street, may be the site of another skirmish, the Battle of Bell o' the Brae, recorded in Blind Harry's poetic account of the hero's life, "The Wallace". Heading northwards from the old centre, up Castle Street, turn right after the motorway bridge on to the A804, Royston Road, and follow it for about a mile and a half to the roundabout where Robroyston Road branches off to the left. About a mile further on, just past the Robroyston housing estate, is one of the country's numerous Wallace memorials, on the old Burgh Muir of Glasgow. Tradition has it that here Wallace was betrayed by Sir John Menteith on 5 August 1305. Believing Menteith to be an ally, the hunted Wallace slept in his house, while his host summoned Edward's soldiers. In order to claim he had not said where the fugitive was, by a pre-arranged signal Menteith turned over a loaf of bread; the soldiers searched the house and took Wallace prisoner. The monument is a tall Celtic cross, with a representation of Wallace's longsword incorporated. The parkland around gives only a vague indication of the forested landscape of seven hundred years ago.

Robroyston is very close to Junction 2 of the M80; join this motorway, heading for the city centre. It soon joins the M8, which you follow through central Glasgow's underpasses towards Paisley. Leave the M8 at Junction 29 (13 miles) and take the A737, signed to Irvine. At the first junction, Linclive Interchange, take the A761 past the Linwood industrial site on to the B789. This leads to Main Road in the little town of Elderslie (3 miles), with pleasant views to hill country northward. Almost at the end of the town is a small park on the left-hand side (easy to park by turning off to the left), with a hexagonal column topped by a crown and set on a base with six carved bronze plaques, showing aspects of the hero's life. One of these is a replica of the plaque at Smithfield, London, the site of Wallace's execution. This monument marks Elderslie's claim to be Wallace's birthplace. Although Wallace's father, Sir Malcolm Wallace, held land here, the birth claim is

St Mungo's Cathedral from the Necropolis, Glasgow

disputed by the very similarly named Ellerslie in Ayrshire. Elderslie is situated on the rising slopes of the Gleniffer Braes ("Keen blows the wind on the braes o' Gleniffer" wrote the local bard, Robert Tannahill), with wide views. It is easy to feel that the young Wallace might have stood here, breathed the upland breezes, and felt that "this is my country".

The alternative birthplace is not far away, across beautiful countryside. Rejoin the road, turning left, and drive through the adjacent town of Johnstone, following the B787 Beith Road through the village of Howwood (about 6 miles), in which you take a very tight left and upwards turn on to the B776 which leads you into the green hills, with tantalising views of faraway mountains. At the rural crossroads of Hall (5 miles) turn right, and a mile later, left towards Lugton, where you join the A735 for Kilmarnock. This is an area of good farmland, and the first town you meet is Dunlop ("Fort by the bend", 3 miles), which has given its name both to a tasty Scottish cheese and to a local veterinary surgeon who also invented the pneumatic tyre. In Kilmaurs (7 miles) turn off to the right on the B751 Crosshouse road and follow it past Knockentiber to the crossing with the B7081 at Crosshouse (two and a half miles). Turn left, and follow the Kilmarnock Road to the second roundabout, where you turn off to the right. Close to the Ellerslie Inn is the now unidentifiable site of the long-abandoned Ellerslie village. At least Elderslie has a monument to support its claim; here there is nothing, apart from "Braveheart steaks" at the Inn. Turning left at the Moorfield roundabout, take the A71 towards **Kilmarnock** (2 miles), and turn off into the town at the first junction. On the outskirts you see a sign: "This is Wallace Country." (Kil- names in Scotland generally mean a cell, or small church, set up by or dedicated to a Celtic saint, in this case St Marnock.)

Just south of the town is Riccarton ("Richard's town") named after Sir Richard Wallace, an ancestor of the patriot, who built a castle here. There is no doubt of the family connections, and the young Wallace was certainly very familiar with this countryside. In his youth the castle was held by his uncle, Sir Adam Wallace. Riccarton claims a famous incident in Wallace's youth. He had been fishing in a local stream, either Simon's Burn or the Cessnock Water, and was approached by six English soldiers who demanded his catch. He offered them half; they refused and tried to grab the lot. Wallace knocked down one, took the man's sword, killed two, and put the others to flight. The whole area here is built over and the only record of the castle is a plaque in the wall to the front of the Riccarton fire station.

Nine miles south of Kilmarnock is the Barnweil monument, built in 1855 to Wallace's memory. From the all-routes roundabout south-east of Kilmarnock, take the A77 towards Ayr, turning left on to the B730 at Bogend (about 6 miles). After a mile take the narrow road to the right, towards Heughmill and Underhills, then after another mile branch left down a steep hill to the crossroads at the foot. The monument is up on the right. It is not normally open but access can be got by arrangement (telephone the South Ayrshire Council's Strategic Services on 01292 282842). The battlemented tower is 60 feet high, giving it a total height above sea level of over 400 feet, with fine views out towards the Irish coast, the mountainous Isle of Arran, with the Argyll hills beyond, and the Galloway Hills to the south. Despite its neglected air, the place is strongly redolent of the mid-Victorian resurgence of Scottish national feeling which brought about this and the other Wallace monuments, including the national monument at Stirling.

Retrace the route to the A77, turning left on to it and branching off at Whitletts roundabout on the A719 into the large town of **Ayr** (9 miles). We are still in Wallace country (though Robert Burns vies with him here as local hero). In July 1297 a number of Scottish noblemen, all opposed to English sovereignty over Scotland, were summarily hanged by the English. Among them was Wallace's uncle, Sir Reginald Crawford. To avenge this, Wallace and his men burned down the building in which the English troops were billeted, in the slaughter known as "the Barns o' Ayr". Ayr has other stories of the young Wallace, including two episodes in which he defeated the English soldiers' prize-fighting champion. Wallace, being well over six feet tall, would certainly have been a formidable adversary.

In the High Street is a memorial Wallace Tower, set up in 1832, and featuring a statue by a local sculptor, James Thom. Not far away, another Wallace statue, with sword held on high, can be seen above a shopfront at the corner of High Street and Newmarket Street. It marks the site of the Old Tolbooth (town jail), where Wallace was held on his way to London and execution in 1305.

On the way out of Ayr on the A77 towards Holmston, you pass above the wooded banks of the river Ayr. If you park and go down into the valley, there is an attractive wooded path by the riverside and down here, walking upstream (a few hundred yards to the right), you come to "Wallace's Cave" and a spring known as "Wallace's Heel", though any direct connection with Wallace is impossible to prove.

Rejoining the A77, which bypasses Ayr, you drive north towards Kilmarnock for a mile or so before turning right on to the A719 for Galston (14 miles). The name here, "Gall's town", means the same as "Wallace's town"; it harks back to the days when the language spoken in this part of the country was Cumbric, an early form of Welsh. Galston has a Wallace legend exactly like the Riccarton one; its Standalane tavern commemorates the hero's words to the would-be fish-robbers: "Though I stand alane, and ye are many, ye shall not have me." The inn building is a modernised 18th-century one. No buildings except ruins, and the occasional much-restored church, survive from Wallace's time. The burnings and destructions of Scottish history have seen to that.

From Galston, the Wallace Trail follows the A71 through Darvel to Strathaven (15 miles). Although the Wallace legend likes to refer to him as "the obscure younger son of a country squire", the Wallaces were a well-connected family on both sides. His mother's Crawford relations were spread across central Scotland as knights and clergymen. At Strathaven (pronounced "Strayven", and meaning "broad valley of the Avon"), the castle and surrounding lands were in possession of the Crawfords. The present castle ruins are 15th century.

From Strathaven, take the B7086 towards Lanark, cutting across wooded hill country that was intensively coal-mined in the 19th century and is full of old railway embankments that nowadays look more like Roman remains (the Romans did prospect here for minerals in the 2nd century AD, before being forced out by the local tribes). You follow the B7086 all the way to the A72, turning right at the junction for Lanark (16 miles). This quiet Clydesdale town (its name, from Cumbric, means "clearing in the wood") has a strong Wallace connection. In the marketplace here there was a fracas with soldiers of the occupying English army when some local urchins made a rude gesture by waggling their fingers behind their backs (it was a popular Scottish practice to pretend that the English had tails). When the angry soldiers chased the boys, Wallace intervened, and the fight that followed left several of them dead. But here too lived the lady who according to tradition was Wallace's wife, though she may only have been a friend, Marion Broadfoot or Braidfute. Lanark in 1297 was the seat of an English-appointed sheriff, Haselrigg by name. The sheriff had Marion arrested and questioned as to Wallace's whereabouts; when she would not speak, he had her executed. Wallace broke into his house that night and killed him, and the English garrison was driven out of the town.

As the anti-English uprising got under way, the woods and valleys of Clydesdale, with the castles and tower-houses of Wallace's Crawford relations, made an ideal centre of operations for the insurgents. But he ranged far and wide – as far south as Galloway – seeking, demanding and sometimes enforcing help in the forms of men, food, and accommodation. Lanark remembers Wallace with a plaque on the site of the house that was Marion's, or perhaps his own, and a statue set in the wall of the prominent St Nicholas Church at the foot of the main street. The ruined church of St Kentigern, surrounded by a graveyard (off Hyndford Road – the A73, signed for Carlisle and the South) may have been where Wallace was

The National Wallace Monument and Stirling Bridge from Stirling Castle

married. Much of the work on the church is of a later date.

From Lanark there is a beautiful cross-country drive through the Southern Uplands, following valleys and tracing the countryside where Wallace and his band moved frequently. Take the A706 north towards Harelaw but turn off right on the A70 towards Edinburgh. At the country village of Carnwath (7 miles) take the A721 and follow it past Elsrickle, over the A702 to meet the A72 at Kirkdean. Follow this road (signed for Peebles and Galashiels). At Lyne, you enter into Tweeddale, with the River Tweed far below on the right. Past Peebles (22 miles) and Innerleithen (9 miles), and now very close to the river, look out for the A707, signed to Selkirk. Along this road you pass Caddonfoot, the ancient mustering place of the Scottish army. Here at the king's command it gathered for forays into England, or in preparation to resist invasion.

Nearing **Selkirk**, bear left across the Ettrick Water and into the little town (11 miles). Centrally located in the Borders area, this was a historic meeting place. Here the leaders of the patriotic struggle met in December 1297, and it may have been on this occasion that Wallace was invested with the title of Guardian of Scotland – charged with maintaining the integrity of the country on behalf of its deposed king, John Balliol. Whilst the parliament may have taken place in the surrounding forest, the little "Forest Kirk" now in the Selkirk town cemetery is, as its memorial plaque confirms, the traditional location. In later years Selkirk became famous for its shoemaking industry, and is still the home of the "Selkirk bannock" advertised by local bakers.

Leaving by the A699 in the direction of St Boswells, look out after about 7 miles for signs on the left to the "Wallace Monument". From the small car park an easy woodland path leads you to a sudden superb view over the winding Tweed valley, overlooked by a giant statue of Wallace. This much-mocked effigy has a certain rugged grandeur despite the crudity of the work. It was erected in 1814 by the Earl of Buchan, who also composed the verse on the plinth; on its unveiling the earl was disconcerted to find some local jokers had put a large pipe into the hero's mouth.

The Wallace Trail then brings you north again. Take the A68 from St Boswells (there is a fine view of the Eildon Hills), then the A6091 past Melrose, to join the A7 south of the woollen capital, Galashiels (5 miles). Follow the A7 north across shapely, bare green hills until you reach the Edinburgh City Bypass, the A720 (35 miles). Follow the Bypass westwards to the junction with the M8 (9 miles), follow the M8 for 3 miles, then turn off for the M9 and Stirling. Leave the motorway at Junction 4 (14 miles) and take the A803 towards **Falkirk**.

Here is the site of the crucial battle which Wallace did not want to fight, and which he lost, on 22 July 1298. Knowing that a large English army was hunting him, he had resolved to avoid a pitched battle, well aware that guerrilla warfare was much more effective. But his position was given away, and a battle was inevitable. Its site is not definite, but southeast of the town is Wallacestone. To reach it, turn off the A803 in Polmont (1 mile) on to the B810, and follow this road past

Polmont station, up to Reddingmuirhead (about 2 miles), where you turn left at the crossroads. Wallacestone is less than a mile down this road. The English army advanced from the east over this ridge, and in the park here is one of the earliest "modern" memorials to the hero, set up on 3 August 1810. In Falkirk, the Victoria Park may partly cover the battleground; it holds the memorial to Wallace's most trusted comrade, Sir John Graeme, who was killed in the battle. The traditional site of his death is commemorated by a drinking fountain; his tomb is by the Old Parish Church, in the centre of Falkirk, where there are other memorials, including the grave of Sir John Stewart, also killed in the battle, and to the Stewarts of Bute who fought with Wallace. After the defeat at Falkirk, Wallace gave up his role as Guardian, though not his part in the struggle. He went abroad as an ambassador for Scotland before returning to continue his campaigns.

Leave Falkirk following signs to the M9 (North) and join it at Junction 6 for a short run to Junction 9, leaving the motorway here to enter Stirling by way of Bannockburn. After Wallace's execution, the position for Scotland seemed utterly hopeless. But here, less than ten years later, the decisive battle to retain Scotland's independence was fought by King Robert I in 1314 (Visitor Centre at the battlefield). Though the battle was fought nine years after Wallace's death, it is not a place to pass unvisited on the Wallace Trail, since it represents the culmination of his dream. The site is an open one; there is also a visitor centre, with an audio-visual display.

Bannockburn Heritage Centre, *Glasgow Road, Stirling; tel 01786 812664* (open daily April–Oct, 10am–5.30pm; Nov–Dec, 11am–4.30pm; March 11am–4.30pm).

Stirling (13 miles), at the gateway of the Highlands, is the linchpin of Scotland. The A91, bypassing the town to the east, will lead you towards the National Wallace Monument, high on the Abbey Craig, north-east of Stirling. These steep slopes saw the high point of Wallace's military career, when with his hastily recruited army of footsoldiers, marshalled on the hillside, he defeated the English feudal host with its heavily armoured knights. It was a remarkable achievement, previously believed to be impossible, and news of it went round

Europe. The armoured knight on horseback was the tank of his time. Follow the signs to the Wallace Monument. It is a steep quarter-mile walk from the car park, with steps at the top, but minibuses are available. At the foot of the path you may see an unfortunate "Braveheart" sculpture, which makes the one at St Boswells look positively distinguished.

The tower itself, of rugged architecture and topped by an open Scottish crown spire, is 220 feet high and the top is reached by 246 narrow steps up a spiral stairway (no lifts). It was completed in 1869, a monument both to Victorian national piety and the stamina of the Victorian visitor, as well as to the hero. On the way up there are halls where you can rest and see an audio-visual presentation of the battle site and parts of Wallace's life (with a replica of his mighty longsword), a "Hall of Heroes" containing portrait busts of a fairly mixed collection of great Scottish men (only men, as many visitors have observed), and a diorama-guide to the splendid view from the open platform at the top. From here you can truly get a sense of the strategic position of this area, so much fought over, with the wide gap between the hills and the castle crouched on its rock in the centre. Old as it is, the 15th-century "old bridge" below you is not the bridge of Wallace's day – that was made of wood.

National Wallace Monument, *Abbey Craig, Stirling; tel 01786 472140* (open daily, Jan–Feb and Nov–Dec, 10.30am–4pm; March–May, Oct, 10am–5pm; June, Sept, 10am–6pm; July–Aug, 9.30am–6.30pm).

Here at Stirling is a fitting place to end the Wallace trail. Return to Glasgow by the M9, then M80 (30 miles) or to Edinburgh by the M9 (40 miles).

TRAIL 3

Where Blackmail Began – Exploits of an Outlaw

Three Days in Rob Roy MacGregor's Country

To follow the trail of Scotland's most celebrated outlaw, we return to Stirling – a good place to start exploring the world of Rob Roy. This famous Highlander lived from 1671 to 1734. At that time, the MacGregors, a clan who claimed descent from the ancient Celtic kings, were hard-pressed by more powerful clans on all sides, the Campbells, the Murrays, the Grahams, causing their lament: "We're landless, landless, landless, Gregarach!" They had to live on their wits, which meant stealing other people's cattle, and their reputation for vanishing with the rustled herds earned them the title "Children of the Mist". Rob Roy was one of the most skilful cattle thieves Scotland has ever bred. But there was much more to him than that. He was an important man in his clan, acting as chief for his under-age nephew for some years. A famous swordsman, he was also a keen Jacobite, who fought for the exiled Stewart kings in three battles. And, when he was outlawed by the men of property, he showed himself to be a Scottish "Robin Hood", who might rob the rich but also spare and help the poor. Above all, he was a master of escape. His exploits in evading the forces of law and order are legendary – but true.

In 1688 King James VII of Scotland and II of England had fled to France, and in his place King William and Queen Mary had been set up in London. In the Highlands of Scotland, still at that time a region where young men were brought up to be warriors as well as farmers, many people wanted James back. It was a troublesome time for the government.

Close to Stirling Castle is a modern (1975) statue of Rob Roy, with the famous phrase put in his mouth by Sir Walter Scott: "My foot is on my native heath, and my name is MacGregor." Driving west from Stirling on the A811, signed for Drymen, as you pass below the castle on its steep rock, think of its small garrison of red-coat soldiers in 1689. Mostly English or German, they were in a foreign land, knowing that the nearby mountains harboured thousands of well-armed, hostile, Gaelic-speaking, plaid-wearing Highlanders.

The road skirts the foot of the Gargunnock Hills; to the right, the valley is wide, flat and fertile, divided into farms. In 1689 it was a mixture of reedy fields and bogland, with the fields close to the villages. Where the B822 crosses (8 miles), turn right, and drive for a short distance to the bridge over the winding River Forth. At this now-tranquil spot, the Fords of Frew, long before the bridge was built, was the first place above Stirling where the river could be forded, an important site for travellers, cattle drovers, armies on the march, anyone who wanted to get past Stirling without being seen. Rob Roy knew it well. In the Jacobite Rising of 1715, he was in charge of the Highland army detachment that guarded the ford against a flank attack by the Hanoverian government's troops, while the Battle of Sheriffmuir was being fought. Two years later, he was being brought as a prisoner down from Balquhidder. He was on horseback, but tied to one of his guards. Night was falling as they crossed the river, and whether by a promised bribe or as a favour returned, the bond was cut, and Rob jumped into the water. Discarding his plaid to be shot at, he swam underwater, letting the current take him, and escaped. The Duke of Montrose, who was present, broke the guard's skull with his pistol-butt in fury. With the construction of the bridge and re-forming of the banks, the fords are now not easy to discern.

Lake of Menteith, the Trossachs

Turn back on the B822 and follow it into Kippen village (one and a half miles). The name means "stump" and, huddled on its stumpy hilltop, about its crossroads, it still has an old-world atmosphere. Three hundred years ago it was much smaller, a group of low, thatched cottages and barns. Near here, one autumn morning in 1690, a band of fifty Highlanders came out from the hills and lay in wait for a great herd of cattle due to be driven eastwards to Stirling. Called out by the men of the next village, Buchlyvie, the Kippen men grabbed their scythes and cudgels and ran up on to Kippen Muir, the higher ground to the west, to face the raiders. They were in a tough spot: if they did nothing, the landowner would blame them. But they were farmers facing trained fighting men. There was a short battle. Rob Roy, the young leader of the raiders, ordered his men to fend off the farmers with the flat of their swords, but soon it became a proper fight, with the inevitable end that some of the men of Kippen were left dead. The MacGregors duly got their cattle and herded them into the hills. Later the beasts would be taken south and sold in England. The Cattle Raid of Kippen was only one of many such encounters, ensuring that there was no love lost between the valley dwellers and the men of the hills.

Follow the B822 up to the T-junction on Kippen Muir (three and a half miles) and get an excellent view of the landscape, including the great level expanse of Flanders Moss, drained in the 18th century by Flemish engineers, but impassable bogland in Rob Roy's day. Beyond it rise ranges of hills, with several distinctive peaks over on the left-hand side. Enfolded within them is one of Scotland's most beautiful districts, the Trossachs. Where the ground rises to the west of Flanders Moss, the **Lake of Menteith** lies in its natural basin. The land around the loch was good farmland, and Rob Roy often came to collect the quarterly rent before the Duke of Montrose's factor, or man of business, arrived. Beyond the loch can be seen the gap in the hills through which the River Forth flows. This was the main gate into MacGregor country. To reach it, drive off to the right down the narrow road, cross the A811 in a right/left zigzag at Arnprior, and follow the B8034 over the river and by the loch to reach the A81 at Port of Menteith (7 miles). If time allows, experience some timeless moments by summoning the island ferryboat here and visiting the ruined monastery on **Inchmahome** (see Trail of Mary, Queen of Scots). Turn left on the A81, then right on to the A821 for Aberfoyle (5 miles).

Not many people read Sir Walter Scott's novels these days, but if you have read his *Rob Roy*, you will know that here is the place with the frowsty inn where the stout Glaswegian Nicol Jarvie set fire to a wild Highlander's plaid. Nowadays it is an attractive tourist village, "capital" of the Trossachs, a centre for fishers, climbers, walkers and relaxers. Its buildings are 18th/19th century. Just to the north, on the right-hand side of the A821, is the Queen Elizabeth Forest Park Visitor Centre, an excellent information point for exploring the area (if you are planning to do the Beginnings of Geology Trail, the two-hour Highland Boundary Fault Walk in the Forest Park will be of interest to you).

Queen Elizabeth Forest Park Visitor Centre, *Aberfoyle, Stirling; tel 01877 382383* (open daily, Easter–Oct, 10am–6pm).

The MacGregor clansmen did not live in the village but in the hills around, their "clachans" or hamlets reached by moorland pathways. These hills are now empty, but the remains of houses can often be seen. In Rob Roy's day there was no police force and the government soldiers were more like an army of occupation than a protection. The Highlanders worked out a neat system of paying themselves and securing a form of order. For a regular payment, a farmer or landowner could be assured that his cattle would not be stolen, nor his harvest stores raided. The old word in Scots for payment is "mail". These underhand payments were known as "black mail". The word has since caught on in a big way. Enforcement was usually strict. Rob Roy MacGregor sometimes travelled scores of miles on foot – as swift and stealthy, and as able to read a trail, as any Pawnee – to retrieve cattle stolen from his "clients" by raiders who had come from further north.

Rob Roy was declared an outlaw by the Duke of Montrose, head of the Grahams, in 1713. The excuse was that he owed the duke money. The uncertainties of life meant that he had several homes at different times. The Rob Roy Trail will take you to two of them. The first is at Inversnaid, high above the side of Loch Lomond. Leave Aberfoyle on the B829, following a scenic route past Loch Ard (between Aberfoyle and Loch Ard is the spot, again described in Scott's *Rob Roy*, where the outlaw's redoubtable wife confronted a government troop). Along this road, on a dark day in November 1716, Rob Roy hustled the Duke of Montrose's factor, and tied him to his horse. The man, Mr Graham of Killearn, was to be held to ransom. They had no time to admire the wooded shores of Loch Ard, or to stroll from Ledard farm (5 miles) up the path to the double waterfall (a pleasant half-hour walk each way on a good track, if you have time). Beyond Kinlochard ("head of the high loch") the road becomes a single track, winding among rocky knolls, and skirting Loch Chon ("loch of the dog") to reach Stronachlachar ("point of the stone-mason", 7 miles) on Loch Katrine. Graham of Killearn was brought here in short order and taken by boat to an island in the loch, still known as "The Factor's Isle". The loch, its level somewhat raised since Rob Roy's time, is Glasgow's main source of water; you can cruise it from Stronachlachar, following the route of the MacGregors' galleys.

Stronachlachar Pier, *Stronachlachar, Stirling; tel 01877 376316 for details of cruises on 'Sir Walter Scott'* (runs May–Sept).

The Rob Roy Trail turns back to the T-junction (half a mile), and along the narrow road to the right to Inversnaid (5 miles), following the north shore of Loch Arklet, artificially raised by a dam at its west end. A mile beyond the loch, where the Snaid Burn joins the Arklet Water, Rob Roy in 1690 built himself a house where he lived until March 1713, when it was wrecked by a troop of soldiers sent by the Duke of Montrose. In 1718 the government paid the MacGregors the tribute of building the Inversnaid Barracks, whose remnants can still be seen although the site is now a farm, as a strong point from which to police the region. (It was for a time commanded by General Wolfe, captor of Quebec, as a young officer, and was manned until the 1790s.) Rob Roy responded by kidnapping its squad of builders. He moved himself and his family to another house. Follow the road to Inversnaid Hotel for splendid views from the banks of Loch Lomond to Ben Arthur and Ben Ime. Lack of roads did not greatly impede the Highlanders of three hundred years ago. They swept down Loch Lomond and the other long lochs of the region in their birlinns (galleys). Here at Inversnaid, where the stream falls into the loch, the poet Gerard Manley Hopkins was inspired to make a famous poem:

This darksome burn, horseback brown,
His rollrock highroad roaring down…

The West Highland Way long-distance footpath is on this side of the loch; follow its well-marked route for about three quarters of a mile northward and you come to "Rob Roy's Cave" above the loch, which he may well have used in times of trouble.

Inversnaid is a dead end, but the return to Aberfoyle gives spectacular views facing east and north. Your next destination is not far as the crow flies, scarcely 20 miles; but the way to it is a roundabout though highly scenic one. Leave Aberfoyle by the northbound A821, known as "the Duke's Road" after the Duke of Montrose who had it built. It leads up and over into the very heart of the Trossachs by the little Loch Achray. Here you are only a mile from the east end of Loch Katrine (to the left); bearing right, among the mountains, with Ben Venue behind and Ben Ledi rising ahead, drive past Brig o' Turk ("Pig's bridge") and along the sloping shore of Loch Vennachar to meet the A84 (13 miles). Two miles on the right is Callander, an attractive tourist town with good hillside walks and a well-patronised visitor centre which focuses on Rob Roy. **Callander, Rob Roy & Trossachs Visitor Centre**, *Ancaster Square, Callander, Stirling; tel 01877 330342* (open daily March–Sept; March–May and Oct–Dec, 10am–5pm; June, 9.30am–6pm; July–Aug, 9am–10pm; Sept, 10am–6pm; Jan–Feb, Sat and Sun only, 11am–4.30pm).

If you venture to see the audio-visual Rob Roy, leave Callander again by the way you came, and shortly enter the winding Pass of Leny, where road and tumbling river twist and squeeze through a narrow gorge. On the left opens out the long boomerang-shape of Loch Lubnaig. Just past the roadside telephone, on the right, is St Bride's Chapel ruin. Here, on the old single-file track, a hundred feet up the hillside, Rob Roy was being escorted as a prisoner in the middle of a troop of soldiers in September 1717. Taking advantage of a momentary gap in the line, he leapt from his horse, scrambled up the craggy slope, and escaped.

Drive on through the village of Strathyre to Kingshouse (13 miles), whose name proclaims that it was once a government way-station and safe house in the heart of the "bad-lands". Take the left-hand turn here on to a minor road signed to Balquhidder ("fodder farm"), about 2 miles further on. In this village Rob Roy was captured in April 1717, asleep in a (long-vanished) house, only to escape his captors at the Fords of Frew. And here in the little graveyard Rob Roy was buried on New Year's Day 1735. After all his battles and exploits, he died at the age of 65 of natural causes, a respectable old age for the times. His wife, Helen, and Coll, one of his sons, also lie here. The grave-slab, appropriate as it seems, with its carved warrior and two-handed longsword, pre-dates Rob himself by some three hundred years. The church is mid 19th century, but the ruins of the old church remain, with the date 1631 carved in the stonework. This itself was built on an earlier church, which in turn covered the grave of a Celtic hermit, Saint Angus. There is a sense of great antiquity in the air here. In the village, Stronvar Country Hotel maintains a small "Bygones Museum" (tel 01877 384698; email stronvar@summer.almac.co.uk).

Driving on westwards beneath the Braes of Balquhidder, on another narrow road liable to have a grassy strip in the centre, you are retracing the route taken by Rob's funeral party, with pipers leading and mourners taking it in turns to carry the bier. Old Scottish funerals were strange mixtures of grief and festivity – at Rob Roy's the crowd was so great that it cost his wife the equivalent of a year's income to entertain them suitably. Two fine hills dominate the route, Ben Tulaichean to the right, Stob a' Choin to the left. A narrow spit separates Loch Voil from the small Loch Doine – at the far side here is Monachyle Tuarach, where Rob Roy was captured at his nephew's house in September 1717, only to escape at Loch Lubnaig.

Just over a mile past the end of Loch Doine, and about 10 miles from Balquhidder is the site of Rob Roy's last home, at Inverlochlarig, built by him around 1720. It is a fine, open site where four glens meet – a tribute to the hardiness of the old Highlanders that they could make their homes in such places. There are few houses on the way to Inverlochlarig today, but in the early 18th century, a large population would have lived in thatched stone houses on the hillsides, with little fields around and black cattle grazing. In summer, they would have moved higher up the slopes to the summer grazing places. The sharp-eyed traveller can still see the evidence of old fields and of houses largely returned to the earth. The peace of today is a peace of desolation; the peace found here by Rob Roy in his last years was that of security among his own people. The past is indeed another country, though here and there we can see more deeply into it.

Once again you are at the end of a road, and must return eastwards towards Balquhidder and Kingshouse, where you turn left on to the A84 and follow it for about 3 miles to **Lochearnhead**. At this water-skiing centre, turn right on the A85, signed for Crieff and **Perth**. Threading through the old earldom of Strathearn, this is a route packed with interest, both natural, historical and scenic. Crieff, then a small town of thatched houses, was a place well known to Rob Roy, as it was the location of a great annual cattle market, the "Crieff Tryst". In 1714, with a whiff of insurrection already in the air, Rob Roy staged a Jacobite demonstration by the town cross at midnight, when he and thirty armed clansmen drank a series of illegal toasts to "King James VIII" and the Jacobite leaders. Nowadays there are frequent bagpipe parades in the town on summer evenings.

If you are interested in malt whisky distilling, there is a chance here to visit the picturesquely situated Glenturret Distillery, established in the 18th century, and well signposted off the A85 to the north of the town.

Glenturret Distillery, *Crieff, Perthshire; tel 01764 656565* (open Feb–Dec, Mon–Sat 9.30am–6pm, Sun 12 noon–6pm; Jan, Mon–Fri 11.30am–4pm).

After Crieff (20 miles), turn left on the A822 and follow the road through the "Sma' Glen", in and out of Glen Almond; then follow the A822 to Dunkeld (17 miles), an attractive tiny cathedral town on the Tay, and turn left up the A9 (exit by the minor road branching left from the A923 Blairgowrie road). About 7 miles north, turn left at Ballinluig on to the A827, signed to Aberfeldy, but stop in Logierait, just across the River

Tummel, on the peninsula formed between it and the Tay. Here was a fortress tower belonging to another grandee whom Rob Roy vexed, the Duke of Atholl. Earlier in that eventful year of 1717, Rob Roy was lured by a false promise of safe conduct from this duke, who promptly had him locked up here. The duke had scarcely finished writing boastful letters to everyone from King George down that he had secured the country's most notorious outlaw, when he was devastated to learn that Rob had escaped. Rob's wife had sent a messenger, and the over-trusting jailer let Rob go to the door to talk to him. In a moment Rob had thrust him aside, mounted the horse brought by the messenger, and was away, riding swiftly west and south to the MacGregor country. The tall memorial here is not to Rob Roy but to the 6th Duke of Atholl.

However, Rob Roy had earlier experience of this region. Aged 18, on 7 July 1689, he had been a member of the Jacobite force, under Viscount Dundee, that had defeated the government army at Killiecrankie, about 8 miles north on the A9 and 3 miles south of **Blair Atholl**. The battleground is preserved, with a visitor centre by the roadside just above the gorge. A clear impression can be got of the place where the Highlanders, throwing aside their plaids and shouting their war-cries, rushed downhill in their saffron-coloured shirts, scattering the redcoats in one devastating charge. The battle was fought in the evening:

> It was past seven o'clock. Dundee gave the word. The Highlanders dropped their plaids. The few who were so luxurious as to wear rude socks of untanned hide spurned them away…In two minutes the battle was lost and won…the mingled torrent of red coats and tartans went raving down the valley to the gorge of Killiecrankie.

So wrote Lord Macaulay. The walks here are inevitably steep and you can see the "Soldier's Leap", allegedly taken by one fugitive across the gorge's narrowest point. But the death of Dundee prevented the Jacobites from following up the victory as no other leader could unite the quarrelsome clan chiefs. After failing to dislodge a regiment of Cameronians from Dunkeld (they melted the lead of the cathedral roof for bullets), Rob, with his father and the other MacGregor clansmen,

went home. The battlefield, owned by the National Trust, is an open site with free access; there is also a visitor centre with information on the natural history of the area as well as on its historic significance.

Crieff town centre, Perthshire

Killiecrankie, NTS Visitor Centre, *Killiecrankie, Pitlochry, Perthshire, PH16 5LG; tel 01796 473233* (open daily April–Oct, 10am–5.30pm).

Given Rob Roy's professional interest in cattle, it is appropriate to link this trail with the Perth Mart. From Killiecrankie follow the A9 south to Perth (32 miles), turning off on to the A85, signed for Crieff, and look out for signs to Perth Mart on the left after 1 mile. This is the centre of great cattle auctions, including the internationally famous Perth Bull sales in February and October, and also of other livestock and farming equipment sales. On market days the people attending are just as interesting as the prize animals, with a wonderful range of styles of tweed suiting. There is a daily animal display in summer. The cattle seen here today bear little resemblance however to the small, scrawny black cattle that Rob Roy drove.

Perth Mart, *East Huntingtower, Perth, Perthshire; tel 01738 474170* (open March–Oct, Mon–Sat 9am–5pm, Sun 10am–5pm; Nov–Feb, daily, 10am–5pm).

Return towards Edinburgh by way of the A9 and M90 roads; this latter will take you across the Forth Road Bridge (no toll southbound) with a spectacular view of the firth and of the great railway bridge on the left.

Recommended Reading: *Rob Roy MacGregor, His Life and Times* by W.H. Murray

TRAIL 4

The Coast of the Silver Darlings

The Herring Trail through some of Scotland's fishing harbours

Of all the fish that swim in the sea
The herrin' it is the fish for me…

So runs the chorus of an old Scottish song, which celebrates all the ways in which a herring can be used. More romantically, they were sometimes called "the silver darlings". Until the 1950s, the seas off Scotland were rich in herring, many of them smoked to produce the succulent kippers that still form part of the traditional breakfast, but also salted and exported in vast quantities. Since then the herring, and many other fish species, have become rarer and more elusive. Many of the little fishing ports round the Scottish coast have given up deep-sea fishing, but a few still maintain a fishing fleet, and in many others the atmosphere of an old port still lingers.

This trail is divided into two, and can be done as a one-day trip from Edinburgh (Part One); or as a two/three-day trip (with Part Two), which can also link in with the Malt Whisky Trail.

PART ONE: THE FIFE PORTS (ONE DAY)

Leave Edinburgh on the A90, signposted for the Forth Bridge (have £1 or the correct change ready as you approach the toll-station). Here two of the world's great bridges cross side by side above a historic waterway. Below for hundreds of years ran the Queen's ferry, established by St Margaret, wife of King Malcolm III, in the 12th century to carry pilgrims to the shrine of the apostle Andrew at St Andrews. On the north side you arrive in Fife, an old province of the Pictish kingdom. Carry on up the M90 for about 4 miles to Junction 3, where you turn off on the A92 for Kirkcaldy. Follow this road to the round-about signed for Kirkcaldy West (14 miles), turn off towards Kirkcaldy, but branch to the left after half a mile at the out-skirts of the town, making towards the sea and Dysart.

Now a suburb, this was once a significant town in its own right and the quiet centre still shows the typical old Scottish tolbooth, or combination of town hall and town jail, in addition to some attractive old houses. In one of these the Dysart Community Centre is a little coffee place cum library for locals and welcomes visitors. Park here or drive down the narrow street nearer to the harbour. From the 16th to 18th centuries, this tiny port was a state-of-the-art harbour exporting coal, hides and fish, and bringing in timber, iron, wine, fine salt and other luxury goods. The tower on the hill is a reminder that trade was vigorously controlled, also that out in that glistening sea lurked pirates of different nationalities – Dutch, English, not to mention Scots.

Leave Dysart (the name means "desert" – this was where St Serf had a hermitage in the 7th century) following main road signs to the A92 and the Tay Road Bridge, but turn right just at the edge of Kirkcaldy town on to the A915 towards Leven. As some of the names in the area ("Coaltown of Wemyss") tell you, you are in former mining country, and the harbour of Methil grew large on coal exports. Bypassing the still-industrial ports of Methil and Leven, follow the A915 through Lundin Links. Just after this resort village, turn right on the side road for Lower Largo (1 mile) to see the home of Alexander Selkirk, whose life story was the model for Daniel Defoe's Robinson Crusoe. A life-size statue of Selkirk is set in the upper wall of a house on the main street.

Returning to the main road, turn on to the A917 at Upper Largo and follow this road to Pittenweem (17 miles). After Leven you are in the picturesque "East Neuk" (corner) of the county of Fife. Reaching the coast at Elie, the trail here threads through a string of delightful old-fashioned towns and villages. There are many places where you can stop and explore, making personal discoveries (like the late 14th-century church of St Monans, so near the sea you can hear the waves break; and with a ship model suspended in its rafters). In summer – for the hardy – there are also fine bathing beaches (also good for sandcastle building).

The first trail harbour is at Pittenweem: follow signs off the A917 into the town and park by the harbour. This is still a working harbour, fronted by well-restored old houses,

Crail harbour, East Neuk of Fife

with fishing nets in piles and fish boxes stacked by the fish-market building. The boats, tubby vessels abristle with masts, derricks, aerials and specialist gear, though often built up over much older hulls, have a purposeful air. Scottish fishing boats are usually green or dark blue – sea colours perhaps to propitiate the dangerous element in which they work. Their names often have a lyrical touch. Pittenweem means "place of the cave", and the cave-shrine of a 6th-century hermit monk, St Fillan, is still preserved as a place of worship in the cliff behind the harbour (open Tues–Sat 10am–5pm, Sun 12 noon–5pm).

Less than 2 miles further along the coast is Anstruther. Its harbour, though larger, has fewer fishing boats, but one of them is the "Reaper", a preserved "Fifie" sailing vessel of a sort once common along the east coast. It belongs to the excellent national Fisheries Museum, built here around an old boat-building yard and richly informative not only of an industry but of a bygone way of life. It is interesting to walk through the period "fisherman's house" with its cosy, cluttered rooms and net loft above. The town's name means "the stream" and the place is built over tunnelled streams that course their way from the rocky slopes to the sea. There is a working lifeboat station to see here, and you can also take a boat trip out to the Isle of

May (its Norse name means "seagull island"), once a dangerous haunt of pirates, now abandoned to the seals and seabirds as a national nature reserve. The trip, contingent on tide times and the weather, lasts four hours. The telephone enquiry line is 01333 310103.

Anstruther, Scottish Fisheries Museum, *The Harbourhead, Anstruther, Fife; tel 01333 310628* (open April–Oct, Mon–Sat 10am–5.30pm, Sun 11am–5pm; Nov–March, Mon–Sat 10am–4.30pm, Sun 2pm–4.30pm).

Five miles east is Crail, perhaps the most picturesque of all these delightful towns. The harbour here is more open, and the air of the place, combined with the red-pantiled houses with their crow-step gables and distinctive architecture, have made it an artists' haven. It was here in the 1930s that a "Little Houses" scheme was launched to preserve the typical style of Scottish town and village house in the face of the spread of bland, identical "modern-style" housing, perhaps convenient but devoid of character. Crail has a Dutch air about it, and Holland was its main trading market. The tolbooth tower bells here have Dutch inscriptions, which translate into English as: "I was cast in the year of our Lord 1520" and "Peter Van den Ghein cast me in the year 1614".

It was the revenues of the North Sea trade that enabled Crail merchants to build their solid houses, which were probably more comfortable when they were built than the draughty castles of the nobility.

Crail Museum and Heritage Centre, *Crail, Fife; tel 01333 450869* (open Easter–Sept, Mon–Sat 10am–1pm, 2pm–5pm).

Part One of the Silver Darlings Trail stops at Crail. You can continue straight into Part Two, or go on to **St Andrews**, 10 miles away, to link in with the Land of the Picts Trail, or return to Edinburgh via the A917 (opportunity to take an inland short cut via the B942), A915, A92 and M90.

PART TWO: THE NORTH-EAST (TWO DAYS)

Note: Much of the territory between Parts 1 and 2 of the Silver Darlings Trail is featured in the Land of the Picts Trail between St Andrews and Aberdeen.

This trail starts at Peterhead, 33 miles north of Aberdeen on the A90 (take the A982 into the town from Invernettie). The prison-like building on the seaward side is indeed a prison, built of the local pinkish granite. The scale of Peterhead harbour shows how large the fishing industry became in the late 19th century. This was a whaling port as well as an inshore and deep-sea fishing town; the Greenland whale fisheries helped to build its wealth. It remains a major fishing port, and the fishmarket can be seen in action on weekday mornings, usually around 8 am. The off-shore oil industry also uses the harbour, where you can see many of the specialised vessels needed to service the rigs and pipelines. There is a Maritime Heritage Centre which covers the history of the fishing industry as well as other aspects of Peterhead's connections with the sea. You can also inspect the lifeboat station.

Maritime Heritage Centre, *The Lido, South Road, Peterhead, Aberdeenshire; tel 01779 473000* (open April–Oct, Mon–Sat 10am–5pm, Sun 12 noon–5pm; telephone for opening times Nov–March).

North of Peterhead, the A90 runs to the right of flat coastal lands past the big North Sea natural gas terminal at St Fergus before veering left into hillier country by the shoulder of Mormond Hill. This is the land of the ploughmen's "bothy ballads", still sung locally. There was a sharp divide between the fisherfolk and the country people, linked only by the fishwives who used to tramp with their creels (wicker baskets) on their backs, loaded with fish to sell in the villages and at the farms.

The road runs straight into Fraserburgh (18 miles), with its big harbour. A handsome Georgian Customs House stands on the right, and there is a great sandy beach backed by golf links. Here is another lifeboat station, as well as much marine activity. There are attractive old buildings in the town, including some with Dutch-style rounded gables from the 1740s, showing again the influence of the North Sea trade.

At the northern tip of the town, Kinnaird Head, stands one of the oldest Scottish lighthouses, built into the remains of an old tower in 1787 by the splendidly named Commissioners for Northern Lights. It is now a lighthouse museum. Looking leftwards, the rocks would in the 19th century have been covered with fish, gutted and spread out, drying in the sun and wind and watched over by the fisher-men's children, whose job it was to keep the seagulls off and to cover up the drying fish if it rained. Dried salt fish was an important export commodity. You may think Fraserburgh, with its spires and towers, is exceptionally well provided with churches – the local landowners in the 19th century, the Frasers, were Catholics and so there are Catholic, Episcopalian and Presbyterian churches. In addition the fisher community, living close to the harbour, was and often still is attracted to tight-knit religious sects like the Plymouth Brethren. Each had its own meeting-house.

Museum of Scottish Lighthouses, *Kinnaird Head, Fraserburgh, Aberdeenshire; tel 01346 511022* (open April–Oct, Mon–Sat 10am–6pm, Sun 12 noon–6pm; Nov–March, Mon–Sat 10am–4pm, Sun 12 noon–4pm).

Westwards from here stretches a wild and cliff-bound coast, with here and there a tiny fishing village squeezed into a niche just above the sea. The older (18th-century) houses of these villages are striking in their colours, the outsides thickly and brilliantly painted to help preserve the rubble walls from salt spray and rain.

Take the coast road, the B9031, from Fraserburgh towards Macduff, past Rosehearty, another fishing community, and diving down deeply into the valley of the Troup Water. Turn right on the short side road for Pennan (2 miles) to see an example of a cliff-foot fishing station with its line of cottages fronting the sea. There is a fine short half-hour walk up on to the bluff to the east, towards Pennan Head, with panoramic views. Four miles on from Pennan is the more dramatically placed Gardenstown, with its tiny rock-surrounded harbour below the cliffs. Built for sailing vessels, these little harbours are too small for modern boats, and the fishermen keep their boats in the larger harbours where fuel supplies, ice chutes and mechanical repairs are available. Many of the cottages nowa-days are used by visitors.

After 5 miles, you join the A98, and a mile further on is another large fishing port, Macduff, founded in 1783, its harbour enlarged in 1877 at the height of the 19th-century herring boom. Across the River Deveron is its "twin-town", the royal burgh of Banff, which has been called "the completest old

Kinnaird Head Lighthouse, Fraserburgh, Aberdeenshire

town in Scotland". In earlier times there was a royal castle here, on the hillside above the sea, but the present building on the site is an 18th-century Adam house. Banff was for long the county town of Banffshire, and an important commercial and social centre. The richer country lairds (landowners) built themselves town houses here, to pass the winter months.

Parking is easy. Starting from the pillared information centre, where town maps are available, walk through High Street and Low Street, and down to High Shore. Many of the houses carry descriptive plaques, and Banff will still give you a feel for town life in the 17th and 18th centuries. The name Duff looms large in these parts – Duff House lies just to the south of the town, an Adam building of 1735 modelled on the Villa Borghese of Rome. It has good collections of paintings and arms and armour, and finely landscaped grounds, including a golf course, stretching along the west bank of the River Deveron. The produce of the sea, from those shore-line hamlets and from the inland farms where the farmhands lived in primitive "bothies" or huts, all contributed to the opulence of the Duffs, who became Dukes of Fife. The house is now part of the National Galleries of Scotland.

Duff House, *Banff, Banffshire; tel 01261 818181* (open April–Sept, daily, 10am–5pm; Oct–March, Thurs–Sun 11am–4pm).

Leaving Banff on the A98, turn right (1 mile) to stay near the coast on the B9139. The fishing village of Whitehills is off to the right; you turn left towards Portsoy, a pleasant little town of typical Scottish dormered appearance, about 6 miles from Banff. Another 6 miles takes you to Cullen, attractively situated among green hills facing the sea, with its disused railway viaduct resembling some Roman monument. Cullen is famed for its local fish soup, known as "Cullen Skink". All along this coast you should be sure of three prime culinary items: fresh fish, grass-fed beef and excellent potatoes. Inland from here is some of the world's best potato-growing country. At Cullen is another stately home, Cullen House, with an attractive 16th-century church close by.

Just out of Cullen, turn right on to the A942, with the golf course and the golden sands of Cullen Bay to the right, and follow the road through a string of small fishing communities, Portknockie, Findochty (its old street full of quaint and colourful fishermen's cottages), Portessie and Ianstown, to Buckie (10 miles), with its big, bustling harbour, where boat-building and repairing is still carried on. Park by the "Buckie Drifter" Maritime Heritage Centre. Inside there is a reconstruction of a quayside scene from the 1920s, with a steam drifter unloading its catch of herrings. The whole story of herring fishing is explained here. There is also a "retired" Orkney-class lifeboat to explore. As you emerge, now highly

Duff House, Banff, Banffshire

knowledgeable on the subject of herring, a stroll to the old fishing village, with its colourful cottages, dating from the 17th century and enlarged in 1723, seems quite in order.

The Buckie Drifter, *Freuchny Road, Buckie, Banffshire; tel 01542 834646* (open Easter–Oct, Mon–Sat 10am–5pm, Sun 12 noon–5pm).

Leave Buckie on the A990, signed for Portgordon, but, where the main road turns away from the sea, look out for a minor road signed to Spey Bay. This road winds inland a little way to a crossroads (turn right) and in 2 miles you reach Spey Bay. Here is a little museum dedicated to salmon fishing: the netting of sea salmon is still practised in various places along the coast. Its traditional approach, using high-prowed boats known as "cobles", contrasts with the high-tech aspects of the deep-sea fishing fleet.

Tugnet Ice House, *Spey Bay, Moray; tel 01309 673701* (open daily, May–Sept, 11am–4pm).

Take the B9104 along the river to join the A96 Aberdeen–Inverness road, and turn right for Elgin. (Just a quarter-mile on the left is the village of Fochabers, where the preserves-making company Baxters has set up a "Highland Village" Visitor Centre, and where there is also a folk museum concerned with farming life.) Nine miles through rich farming country take you to Elgin.

At Elgin you can link with the Malt Whisky Trail. But a final fling of the Silver Darlings Trail is possible, if you take the A941 out to Lossiemouth. This is a pleasant evening drive, past the ruins of Spynie Palace, once the residence of the Bishops of Moray, to the sea, where you view the mountains of Sutherland across the Moray Firth. Lossiemouth has a Fisheries and Community Museum, and there is an easy walk along the shoreline towards the tall Covesea Lighthouse, guarding ships against the offshore rocks or skerries.

Lossiemouth Fisheries and Community Museum, *Lossiemouth, Moray; tel 01343 813772* (open Easter–Oct, Mon–Sat 9.30am–5pm).

TRAIL 5

Royal Scotland

One day in Dunfermline–Falkland–Scone–Stirling. Half a day in Edinburgh

From 1032 to 1603 Scotland was a unified kingdom, with its own monarch. For most of this time there was no fixed "capital", though Edinburgh was, from the 13th century on, the largest town. After 1603, when King James VI of Scotland also inherited the throne of England and departed for London, Scotland saw very little of her kings or queens for more than two hundred years. James VI came back for a single short visit in 1616 and Charles I came to Edinburgh for a coronation ceremony in 1633. Charles II, a refugee fighting for his throne, was in Scotland from 1650 to 1651. After that, no reigning monarch came to Scotland until 1822 when King George IV made a visit to Edinburgh, although there were two unofficial visits by members of the exiled Stewart line, including the capture of Edinburgh by Prince Charles Edward in 1745 (see Trail of Prince Charlie). In 1853, Queen Victoria purchased Balmoral Castle in Aberdeenshire, and became a regular summer visitor, setting up a pattern which is maintained by the present royal family.

PART ONE: DUNFERMLINE–FALKLAND–SCONE–STIRLING

To get the most out of the Royal Scotland Trail, leave the Edinburgh part to the last. Make a morning start from there, leaving the city on the A90 Forth Bridge road, cross the bridge (toll) and turn off to the left at Junction 3 (15 miles), following the A907 through Halbeath into Dunfermline (3 miles). There are several car parks and parking streets in the town centre (time-related meter payment). Park in Canmore Street, near to the well-signposted abbey and equally convenient for the town centre, up on the right of the abbey (worth seeing for its historical placards and the incredibly florid Town Hall).

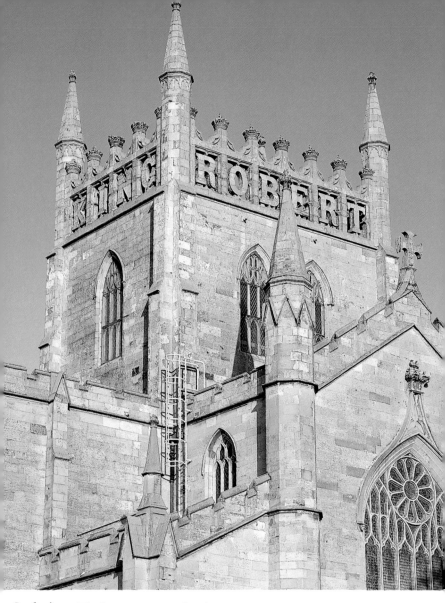

Dunfermline Abbey, Fife

The king sits in Dunfermline toun,
Drinking the blood-red wine…

So begins the old ballad of 'Sir Patrick Spens' – a reminder that this place was the main home of some of Scotland's Celtic kings. Looking downhill towards Dunfermline Abbey, you will see that the central tower has the words "King Robert the Bruce" built into its open-work top, to tell the world that he is buried here. In 1068, King Malcolm III (also known as

Canmore, the "Great Chief" and the man who defeated Macbeth) married the Saxon Princess Margaret. Margaret, later canonised, founded a Benedictine Priory here in 1072, which later became an abbey in the reign of her son David (1150), and the western part of the church dates from then. Eight kings and four queens of Scotland are buried here. The eastern part of the church is a 19th-century building; the door from it to the old nave takes you 700 years in a single step. Set between the two incised eastern pillars of the old nave, the tomb of Bruce is covered by a memorial brass mounted in porphyry (his body, wrapped in gold-threaded cloth, was found during building work in 1818 and re-interred).

Just by the abbey are the ruins of the royal palace, where the unfortunate King Charles I was born in 1600, four years after his sister Elizabeth, who became the 'Winter Queen' of Bohemia. The hillside site is a dramatic one; both palace and abbey needed massive foundations on the steep slope. The site is partly an open-access one, but a ticket is needed to get inside the ruins. The single remaining wall of the palace, with its fine masonry window-frames, dates from the reign of James V in the early 16th century. Abbey and palace overlook the fine Pittencrieff Park, given to the town by its most famous non-royal son, the steel-king Andrew Carnegie, born here in 1835 (he has a Birthplace Museum here). Another celebrated connection is that William Wallace's mother is buried in the abbey churchyard – a thorn tree is said to mark the spot. The royal and other historic connections of the town are displayed in the "Abbot House", the medieval gatehouse to the abbey.

Dunfermline, Royal Palace and Abbey, *Dunfermline, Fife; tel 01383 739026* (open April–Sept, daily, 9.30am–6pm; Oct–March, Mon–Wed and Sat 9.30am–4pm, Thurs 9.30am–12 noon, Sun 2pm–4pm).

The Abbot House, *Maygate, Dunfermline, Fife; tel 01383 733266* (open daily, 10am–5pm; closed Christmas and New Year's Day).

Carnegie Birthplace, *Moodie Street, Dunfermline, Fife; tel 01873 724302* (open April–Oct, Mon–Sat 11am–5pm, Sun 2pm–5pm).

Leave Dunfermline the way you came on the A907, cross over the M90, and continue on the A92, signed for Tay Road

Bridge past the new town of Glenrothes, and turn left on the A912 at Muirhead, for Falkland (28 miles).

Located just on the edge of the Lomond Hills, Falkland was a hunting ground for wild deer and boar. On the East Lomond hill that rises above, there is an old Pictish fort where Macduff, Thane of Fife, had a castle. Falkland passed into the ownership of the Stewarts, who became the royal family of Scotland in 1371, with the accession of King Robert II. He was followed by the weak Robert III, whose heir apparent, David, Duke of Rothesay, was starved to death here in 1402 by his uncle Murdoch, Duke of Albany. Falkland became a favourite hunting lodge for the later Stewart kings. The palace as it now is was built between 1453 and 1541, between the reigns of James II and James V. James V is perhaps most associated with it. As a boy of 16, held in the control of the ambitious Earl of Angus, he escaped from here to ride through the night to Stirling and assert his own authority. Later, it was from here that he set out on many of his secret amorous expeditions; he had the "real tennis" court built in 1539, and after a strange physical and mental collapse, he died here in 1542. A Scottish chronicler described how, having forecast the ruin of the Stewarts under his baby daughter Mary to his assembled courtiers, he "turned his face to the wall" and spoke no more.

Set in the tiny old town of Falkland, the palace shows a Scottish adaptation of late Renaissance styles learned from France; the twin towers at the entrance are smaller versions of those at Holyroodhouse in Edinburgh. The palace was partly destroyed by fire in the 17th century, but much remains and has been expertly restored, including the Chapel Royal. The gardens, laid out in the 1530s, have also been restored. The departure of King James VI to England left the little palace high and dry – a monument to the successive Jameses who built and loved it.

Falkland Palace and Garden, *Falkland, Fife; tel 01337 857397* (open April–Oct, Mon–Sat 11am–5.30pm, Sun 1.30pm–5.30pm).

The old Town Hall has an exhibition on Falkland's history and, of course, a shop. The brief walk round the old town centre is pleasant; if you have the time for a longer stroll, walk to the viewpoint on the top of the East Lomond. Just over a mile south of Falkland on the A912, turn right after the Purin Farm turn, and drive a mile and three quarters up the narrow road to the radio masts. From here an easy path goes up the shoulder of the hill to the panoramic viewpoint on the top. Here there are also the earthworks of a prehistoric fort. Lomond means "beacon hill", and a signal fire here would be visible across a wide sweep of country.

Leave Falkland on the A912, heading northwards for Perth (20 miles), turning left on to the A91 near Strathmiglo, and right on to the A912 where it resumes at Gateside. Join the M90 at Junction 9, follow Dundee signs at Junction 10, and A93 Blairgowrie signs at the end of the motorway (here you sweep across the River Tay on a high bridge). Still following the A93 and passing to the east side of Perth, continue for about 2 miles to Old Scone, and turn off to Scone Palace. Despite the name, this is not a royal palace but the home of the Earls of Mansfield.

Scone, however, has a central place in the royal tradition of Scotland (the name, pronounced "Scoon", may mean "hump" or "mound"). When the Picts and Scots were united under King Kenneth MacAlpin around AD 843, this was the place where kings were formally invested. The ceremony, originally pagan, was given a Christian gloss. The ancient "Lia Fail" (Stone of Destiny), brought by the Scots from Ireland in the 6th century, was brought here and kept in the abbey church. Here, based on a contemporary description, is how Alexander II, as a boy of 8, was crowned king in 1249:

> *The Stone of Destiny, placed beneath a tall Celtic cross, was spreadwith silk embroidered in gold. The procession approached it from the abbey. The young prince sat, as the Earl of Fife placed the crown on his head and the Bishop of St Andrews performed the Act of Consecration. The moment the boy became king was when he was presented with a wand by the chief bard, or ollave. The earls of Scotland cast their mantles down before him. Then an aged sennachie approached, fell to his knees, and recited the pedigree of the young king in Gaelic…all the way back to "Iber the first Scot, son of Gaithel Glas, son of Neoilus, King of Athens, begotten of Scota, daughter of the Pharaoh Chenthres, king of Egypt."*

Falkland Palace and Gardens, Falkland, Fife

It was an open-air ceremony, whose critical moment was accomplished, not by the bishop, but by a man who exemplified the tradition of the Druids. The last time it was performed was in 1651, when Charles II was crowned King of Scots here.

The abbey was founded in 1114, and it was from here that the Stone of Destiny was removed by the men of Edward I of England in 1296, along with other Scottish treasures and documents. The house of Scone Palace, built in the early 19th century, stands on the former abbey site. The crowning-place is just to the north, where a fragment of the old parish church is now the mausoleum of the Murray family. The house has few specifically royal mementoes, though some of its 16th-century tapestries are supposed to have been made by Queen Mary when she was imprisoned in **Loch Leven Castle**. The locality here is called Old Scone since the Earl of Mansfield, in 1818, had the village razed to the ground because it spoiled his view, and the inhabitants transferred out of sight, more than a mile away, to "New" Scone. The resultant park is very fine, with magnificent trees.

Scone Palace and Park, *Scone, Perth; tel 01783 552300* (open early April–late Oct, daily, 9.30am–5.15pm).

Nearby **Perth** was favoured over Edinburgh by several early kings, who held numerous parliaments here. The important treaty with Norway, handing the Hebrides over to Scotland, was signed here in 1266. King James I was murdered here in February 1437 at the Blackfriars monastery, and a botched kidnap attempt was made on James VI at Gowrie House here in 1600, but nothing remains of these buildings.

Drive across the city to join the southbound A9, signed for Stirling, or return to Junction 11 of the M90, turn right on to the motorway, signed for Crianlarich and Inverness, and turn left on to the A9 for Stirling at the end of the short spur of motorway. The A9 becomes the M9 at Dunblane; you turn off for Stirling (31 miles) at the first Junction, No 10, and follow the A84 into the town, turning off right to climb to the large car park by the castle.

Stirling Castle, the last castle to be captured from the Scots by Edward I in 1302 and the last to be reclaimed by them in 1314, looks squat and low on its steep crag, 340 feet above the plain below, until you get inside, when the buildings take on a grander appearance. The strategic location meant that this was always a castle held by, or for, the king. There is no doubt that it is a fortress, constructed to be as impregnable as possible, but surprisingly the first thing you notice inside is a palace. Nothing shows more clearly the insecurity of Scottish royalty in the 15th and 16th centuries than that they chose to build themselves a Renaissance dwelling in this inconvenient, windy place behind its massive battlements.

Stirling was often a bolt-hole (see Trail of Mary, Queen of Scots). Here a king could feel confident, with his own men about him, and it was here that King James II stabbed the Earl of Douglas to death in February 1452. James II and James V were both born in Stirling Castle, and young James VI spent much time here during the unrest following his mother's forced abdication. The palace complex includes the Chapel Royal (for which some fine church music was written by James IV's court composer Robert Carver), the Great Hall and royal apartments, including the room where Douglas was murdered and his body pitched from the window. Restoration of the palace buildings has been controversial; you will see why as soon as you glimpse the painted walls, said to be based on the original, but making the Great Hall resemble a sort of Victorian summer house.

Stirling Castle, *Stirling; tel 01786 450000* (open April–Sept, Mon–Sat 9.30am–5pm, Sun 10.30am–4pm; Oct–March, Mon–Sat 9.30am–5pm, Sun 12.30pm–4pm).

Stirling town has numerous other historic buildings and is featured in a number of other trails (see Rob Roy and Mary, Queen of Scots). From here you return to Edinburgh. If you have already paused to see the battlefield of Bannockburn, follow the A9, then the A872 towards Junction 9 of the M9, in the direction of Edinburgh. Otherwise park at the Heritage Centre on the right-hand side, which is at the edge of the battle site. Here is a modern equestrian statue of King Robert I, also the interpretive centre which explains this most crucial battle of Scotland's history, fought across what is now a largely built-up area, on 23–24 June, 1314.

Proof of legitimate descent is always desirable in kings, though many have reigned without it. In the case of Robert Bruce, who had himself crowned King of Scots in 1306 with no-one's leave but his own (though backed by some key people including both bishops and earls), he could prove he was descended from the second daughter of David, Earl of Huntingdon, younger brother of King William I of Scotland. This was about as near to the old royal line as anyone could claim to be. William I himself was descended from Kenneth

MacAlpin, first king of both the Picts and Scots, and from him the misty thread goes back to "Iber the first Scot". When Bruce's son David died with no legitimate heir, the nearest claimant to the throne was Robert, the hereditary Steward of Scotland. His mother was Marjorie, daughter of Bruce by his first marriage. Thus the Stewarts, through these two crucial female connections, could claim to be linked with one of the oldest royal lines of Europe.

From here, return to Edinburgh via the M9 (30 miles).

PART TWO: ROYAL EDINBURGH

During the early 1590s, in one of the narrow alleys, or closes, off Edinburgh's High Street, King James VI and a little group of courtiers took refuge from a sudden noisy demonstration (the Edinburgh city mob was always volatile). James was a complex man, much underrated as a monarch. He was brave enough to master his fright, but could not control his physical reactions. Huddled in the close, he was mortified to find that he had soiled his breeches. The incident shows how close were the monarchs of Scotland to the people they ruled. The manners and customs of the country did not run to remote splendour.

It was not an easy business being a Stewart king. James VI was ten generations away from his ancestor Robert Bruce; eleven generations later, Queen Victoria would claim a somewhat erratic descent from him. James had survived several serious kidnap attempts. His mother, Queen Mary, had fled the country after a forced abdication and had been executed in England. His grandfather had died in a nervous collapse at the age of 35. His great-grandfather was killed in battle against the English. His great-great grandfather had been assassinated after a rebellion headed by his own son. His great-great-great-grandfather had been killed by an exploding cannon while fighting the English. His great-great-great-great-grandfather had been assassinated in a coup led by his own relations.

The relationship between the Scots and their monarchs was often difficult. The crown was respected, even venerated; its wearer, however, was seen as distinctly human. Even the famous Declaration of Arbroath, made to the Pope in

1320, stated that if the king should fail to defend the country's independence, then the people would find another king. (This was a most unusual statement for its time.)

These are some thoughts to bear in mind as you make your way along the 'Royal Mile' from castle to palace, formed by successive streets and passing the sites of Parliament, of the High Court, of the old Tolbooth or city jail, the High Kirk of St Giles, and the High Cross from where royal proclamations were made (the present platform around it dates from 1885).

Despite the seventeen kings between James VI and Malcolm Canmore, the memory of two queens is dominant. At the castle, it is Queen Margaret, consort of Malcolm, whose presence is also felt in Dunfermline. The tiny 12th-century Romanesque chapel, oldest surviving building on the castle rock, is sometimes said to be her own oratory or prayer-place, part of the new royal hunting lodge established on the old fortified site. More probably it was built in her memory by her son David I. It was in Edinburgh Castle that, on her deathbed in 1093, she heard the news of her husband's death fighting the English; from here her body was taken back to Dunfermline.

The kings tended to use Edinburgh Castle more as a treasury, prison and military depot than as a home: it was Edinburgh's equivalent of the Tower of London. It was not until the time of James III (reigned 1460–88) that a suite of royal apartments was built, much changed by James IV, who also built the Great Hall. Only in troubled times did they live in the castle. James II, who became king at the age of 6 in 1437, was once, when still a child, smuggled out of the castle in a clothes basket during a power struggle between the governors of Stirling and Edinburgh Castles. At the age of 10, he was present at the gruesome "Douglas Dinner" of 1440, when the teenage Earl of Douglas and his younger brother were dragged away from the supper table to have their heads cut off in the courtyard outside. The flamboyant James IV probably made most use of the castle and its hall: he was a patron of the arts, encouraging bagpipe music as well as the latest French fashions. Here too in Queen Mary's Apartments can be seen the room where James VI was born (see Trail of Mary, Queen of Scots). James himself preferred his new palace at Dunfermline.

In the Crown Chamber are the "Honours of Scotland", the hallowed items which affirm its status as a kingdom – the crown, worn by James V at his coronation, is believed to incorporate an older crown going back to the coronation of David II (1329), the first Scottish king to be crowned with full papal unction. Here too is the Stone of Destiny, whose association with Scottish kingship disappears into the mists of time. Both the "Honours" and the Stone have had chequered careers and their survival is remarkable.

Edinburgh Castle, *Edinburgh; tel 0131 225 9846* (open daily, April–Sept 9.30am–6pm; Oct–March, 9.30am–5pm).

The saintly Margaret also played a part in the beginnings of the Palace. One of her treasures was a piece said to be of the true Cross. This gave its name to Holyrood ("holy cross") Abbey, also founded (1128) by the pious David, where it was kept. As Edinburgh grew in importance, so did the abbey prosper, and like Dunfermline it had a well-appointed guest-house for important visitors. It was King James IV who turned this into a royal palace, and its oldest surviving buildings date from his reign in the early 1500s. Masterful figure as he was, it is his grand-daughter Mary whose memory presides within this part of the palace (See Trail of Mary, Queen of Scots).

Holyrood Palace in its present form dates largely from the late 17th century, when it was restored and enlarged by the architect Sir William Bruce. As Duke of York and Albany, the future James VII lived here for three years as commissioner for his brother, Charles II. The palace was refurbished and extended (1670–1688) with a new tower-block in the south-west corner to balance the previously somewhat lopsided facade; Bruce was both sensible and sensitive in matching the style of the 100-year-old towers on the north-west side, though to the eye of the 1670s they must have looked dreadfully old-fashioned. The interior is less "Scottish"; Dutch artists and wood-carvers, and English plasterers, are responsible for its ornate but heavy, rather Dutch-looking style. One of its curiosities is the series of paintings of Scottish kings in the Long Gallery. These were done by a Dutch painter, Jacob de Witt. No doubt he was advised on their appearance by local antiquaries; nevertheless the effect is mildly comic.

By the side of the palace are the ruins of the Chapel Royal, formerly part of the abbey. The most extraordinary scenes were enacted here in December 1688, at the time of the "revolution" when James VII (as James II of England) fled from London to France. The ever-volatile Edinburgh mob broke into the palace and wrecked the Catholic chapel set up in the old council chamber. Hoping for loot, they broke open the tombs of the Scottish kings in the old abbey and tossed the bones about. For nearly a hundred years the despoiled tombs remained open and neglected, a forlorn spectacle for visitors to come and gaze at.

Palace of Holyroodhouse, *Canongate, Edinburgh; tel 0131 556 7371* (open April–Oct, daily, 9.30am–6pm; Nov–March, daily, 9.30am–4.30pm).

Though this Trail focuses on the time of the Stewarts, a more contemporary royal link is to be found in the former Royal Yacht, *Britannia*, now berthed at Edinburgh's port of Leith, with its staterooms open to visitors.

TRAIL 6

Official Scotland at Work: The Parliament and the High Court

Half a day, or less, in central Edinburgh

Scotland's Parliament sits in the very centre of Edinburgh, having borrowed the Assembly Hall of the Church of Scotland whilst its own new building is under construction. Accountability of the Parliament to the people is deemed very important, and visitors are welcomed. Entry is of course free. The visitors' gallery is reached not from the front door, but from high up on the side of the building, with easy access from the Lawnmarket (Royal Mile) via the alleyway of Mylne's Court, and a long climb from below. There are 400 seats for visitors, and at most times there are seats available. For important debates, however, the gallery fills up quickly. There is a quick, friendly but efficient security procedure before you are admitted into the gallery above the debating chamber, whose seats are laid out in a wide semi-circle round the presiding officer's desk. The effect is bright and intimate – there are 129 members (MSPs) though it is rare to see all of them in the chamber at once. Much work is done in committees.

The Parliament has control over Scotland's internal affairs, though its revenue-raising powers are very limited. Scotland also sends members to the Parliament of the United Kingdom in London, and to the European Parliament in Brussels. The tradition of debate in Scotland, nurtured in the country's older universities, is vigorous and often vehement. In the course of a debate, as successive members rise, it is intriguing to listen to the many different versions of the "Scottish" accent, between the Shetland Islands and Galloway. The Parliament has yet to be called the best theatre in Edinburgh, but since its establishment in 1999 it has rapidly become a commanding element in the country's life.

Some visitors are misled by the existence of the Parliament's "visitor centre" some little way off, at the corner of George IV Bridge and the Royal Mile, close by the High Kirk of St Giles. This centre is an information point, exhibition and

Statue of David Hume outside the High Court of Justiciary, Edinburgh, with the High Kirk of St Giles in the background

shop. When the new parliament building is complete, it will be integrated into the site. It is useful to check in advance whether Parliament is in session or not.

The Scottish Parliament, *Edinburgh; tel 0131 278 1999* (sitting times are usually: Mon 2.30pm–5.30pm, Tues–Thurs 9.30am–5.30pm, Fri 9.30am–12.30pm).
The Scottish Parliament Visitor Centre, *George IV Bridge, Edinburgh; tel 0131 348 5000* (open all year, Mon–Fri 9.30am–5pm, July–Sept, Sat 9.30am–5pm).

Very near the Parliament's Visitor Centre is the centre of Scotland's legal system. The old Parliament House, round the corner, in the courtyard by St Giles, is where the Court of Session, Scotland's supreme court, sits. It judges civil cases and all appeals. There are 27 judges, "Lords of Session", headed by the Lord President and the Lord Justice-Clerk. Much of the Court of Session's work is based on intensive legal detail, as in adjusting Scottish law to European law. Admission is granted to public sessions, subject to available seating.

More dramatic confrontations tend to happen across the road in the building of the "High Court of Justiciary", easily identified by the seated statue of the philosopher David Hume on the pavement outside it. The same law lords are its chief judges. Here is where important criminal charges are dealt with. Barristers in Scotland are known as advocates, and cross-examinations are conducted in a no-nonsense manner. The flamboyant style of advocacy is no longer in great vogue, but it has not quite disappeared. Many aspects of Scotttish law are distinctive, and one is unique – the "third verdict". When a jury – fifteen people – is not convinced of guilt, but is not too sure about innocence either, it can return a verdict of "Not Proven". The effect is similar to that of a "Not Guilty" in that the accused is then released, but a point has been made.

At highly publicised trials, public seats are taken up very quickly, but often it is possible to walk in. The reception desk will tell you what trials are taking place. In visiting these official and security-conscious sites, you need to note the rules, including that of "no photography".

The High Court of Justiciary, *Lawnmarket, Edinburgh; telephone for general enquiries 0131 225 2595.*

Lawyers in Parliament Hall, Edinburgh

Trail 7

The Glen Ogle Trail – Walking on the C & O Road

Half a day, from Lochearnhead (See Rob Roy Trail) or close by. A 5-mile walk climbing about 500 feet. Time: allow 3 hours. Sturdy walkers can do it in less, but why hurry? Walking shoes or boots should be worn. No climbing or scrambling is needed, but there are many stiles.

Until the 1960s, Scotland had a much larger rail network than the present one. Some of the most scenic routes were closed down at that time. One of these was the eastern section of the C & O, nothing to do with the USA's Chesapeake & Ohio, but the Callander and Oban Railway. This line made a link between Edinburgh and the west-coast port of Oban, by way of Stirling and Callander. (Its western arm, from Crianlarich to Oban, remains in use.) The C & O route was hilly, and one of the steepest sections was up the short Glen Ogle, a deep groove cut by Ice Age glaciers. In 5 miles, the line rises some 500 feet, its 1 in 60 gradient a heavy task for the steam engines of the time when the rails were laid in 1870. The line rarely paid its way and the track was lifted in the 1960s.

Walking up the old trackbed, it is possible to visualise the handsome trains of the Caledonian Railway, with their bright blue locomotives and pink-and-brown carriages, puffing their way slowly up the rock-strewn hillside just where you are now walking. The fireman would be busy shovelling coal, the driver keenly looking out for the signals of Glenoglehead Crossing, 945 feet up, where a southbound train might be waiting its turn to occupy the single track. Meanwhile, as steam drifted past their windows, the passengers, bound for Oban or the Western Isles, could look out from comfortable compartments or the luxurious 12-wheeled dining car, as the scenery moved steadily past them at 15 miles an hour. Coming downhill was another matter!

Nowadays, old rail tracks, with their carefully graded uphill stretches, make good walking paths, and Scotland has many of these. This is one of the most spectacular, taking in the 12-arched Glenogle viaduct, which bridges a deep hollow below the cliffs of Sgorrach Nuadh (2,161 feet). Long before the railway, this was a strategic route for cattle drovers heading south (and cattle rustlers heading north). Many a herd of bellowing black cattle was driven down the glen on its way to the great annual cattle fair at **Crieff**.

The start and finish of the walk is at Lochearnhead, on the A84. A small village, it is well provided with amenities for visitors and has a bustling water sports centre on Loch Earn. You set off from the village car park (on the A85 Perth road), and walk back through the village, turning right by the A84, signed for Crianlarich. Down here you see the remains of another dismantled railway, built westwards from Perth to link up with the Oban line. The station, up a road on the left-hand side, is now a scouting centre. Just at the entrance to this road, the Glen Ogle trail sign tells you to branch off to the right. The opening section of the trail is quite steep as the path climbs towards the old railway line, but you will be rewarded by increasingly wide views as you rise higher. The arrow signs of the trail guide you on a zigzagging course through fields, over a stile, up a set of wooden steps, over an old dry-stone wall (these walls, built of local stone without mortar, are typical field and farm boundaries found all over the Highlands), another stile and more steps, until you come to the trackbed. Follow its gentler gradient to the right as it climbs along the side of the glen. Here you can see the tall, gnarled Scots pines, remnants of the Caledonian Forest which once covered this now largely treeless landscape. The viaduct has no wall on its left side; care is needed while crossing it, but it lends a certain zest to the walk. The rail-track cuts its way here through an ancient landslide, a tumble of old rocks and glacial debris in which the steamer-type whistle of the locomotives used to echo. It goes on past the little Lochan Lairig Choile ("loch of the wooded hollow"), but about half a mile beyond the viaduct, just after a bridge over a moorland stream, the way-mark shows the point where you leave the trackbed to follow a rough section of path down to the little bridge over the Ogle Burn (Ogle itself is thought to mean "high place"). The path then bends left to take you across and above the A85 road. As you come back to the trees that grow around the village, at the sheltered foot of the glen, the path crosses the river by a foot-bridge and leads you back towards the main road, where you retrace your steps to the car park.

From Lochearnhead, you can travel east via the A85 to Perth, or south via the A84 (see Rob Roy Trail) towards **Stirling**, and **Edinburgh** via the M9.

Trail 8

Lochs and Monsters

One day, from Inverness

The tradition of the water horse, or "water kelpie", is a very old one in Scotland, probably reaching back to pagan times when rivers and lochs were seen as controlled by a resident spirit (the basis of many river names, including Dee, Deveron, Lochy, is a word meaning "goddess"). In Christian times, from around AD 600 on, this primitive spirit has been "diabolised" as an agent of Satan, supposed to take the form of a horse. This may be because there were herds of wild horses on the Scottish hills until the 16th century. There are many stories of travellers way-laid by the kelpie and dragged to their deaths in the water. In some stories, by making the sign of the Cross, the victims were able to drive the creature away. In a land where there were many fords and – until the 18th century – very few bridges, and sudden floods were common, rivers were dangerous. The lochs were often used for transport, in vessels ranging from fine galleys to leaky patched-up tubs. Sudden squalls were always a hazard.

It is from circumstances such as these that the monster legends have grown. None is more famous than that of Loch Ness. This trail will take you into the land of three loch-based "monsters", each with a Gaelic name: An Niseag ("Nessie") of Loch Ness, An-t-Seileag ("Shiela") of Loch Shiel, and Morag, the beast of Loch Morar, with a side-trip to Loch Arkaig, whose monster has not been named. Even if you do not see a monster, you will pass through some of the finest scenery of the West Highlands.

Starting from Inverness, drive south on the A82 Fort William road. After about 6 miles through pleasant wooded countryside, you come to a stretch of open water at Dochgarroch. This is the north end of Loch Ness, known as Loch Dochfour, separated from the main loch by a narrows. From Lochend the view opens up as your road runs along a steep and sometimes precipitous hillside, in a long valley that runs dead straight in a south-west/north-east direction. You are

in Glen More, the "great glen", an ancient geological fault-line. The slope on which you are driving falls a further 700 feet beneath the waters of the loch, in a gigantic V-shaped depression.

Urquhart Castle, Loch Ness, Inverness-shire

Loch Ness is the largest body of fresh water in Britain, with a volume of 7,500 million cubic metres. You would have to voyage more than fifty miles out to sea before the sea-bed reaches a comparable depth to this huge trench. On the section of the road to Drumnadrochit, there are fine open views of the loch. A tiny road climbs off to the right to Abriachan, once celebrated as a place of illicit distilling. At Drumnadrochit ("ridge of the bridge"), 15 miles from Inverness, there is the "official" Loch Ness Monster Exhibition. Here you will find a wealth of information on the loch, its surroundings, and on the various expeditions and "sightings" associated with the monster.

The first recording of a Ness monster is in the "Life of St Columba", written in the 7th century. On his way to meet the King of the Picts, the saint was confronted by a monster in the River Ness (not the loch), which he dispelled by making the sign of the Cross and ordering it to be gone. Nothing is then recorded for more than a thousand years until some local newspaper reports of 1933, when travellers along the newly made motor road claimed to see a "Strange Spectacle on Loch Ness". Judge for yourself from the evidence!

Loch Ness Monster Visitor Centre, *Drumnadrochit, Inverness-shire; tel 01456 450573* (open March–June and Sept–Oct 9.30am–5.30pm; July–Aug 9am–7.30pm; Nov–Feb 10am–3pm).

On the south side of the bay at Drumnadrochit are the ruins of Urquhart Castle, once a major royal fortress controlling passage through the Great Glen. Apart from its own historical and architectural interest, it offers an excellent vantage point and several "monster" sights have been made from it. West of the castle, by the road, is the memorial cairn to John Cobb, who died here on 29 September 1952 when his boat broke up in attempting to break the world water speed record.

Urquhart Castle, *Drumnadrochit, Inverness-shire; tel 01546 450551* (open April–Sept, Mon–Sat 9.30am–5.15pm, Sun 10.30am–4.45pm; Oct–Mar, Mon–Sat 9.30am–4.30pm, Sun 12.30pm–3.30pm).

Ten miles on is Alltsaigh. If you park at the Youth Hostel here (on the left, just by the loch) and scramble up the banks of the Allt ('river') Saigh, you will see the history of the route through the Great Glen. From the modern road bridge at the foot, you come to an older (19th-century) stone bridge of the previous road, and the even older (18th-century) bridge of the old "military road" above that; and finally to another modern bridge that carries the track cut to gain access to the forested high slopes.

At the end of the 24-mile-long loch is Fort Augustus. The fort here, built in 1729, was part of a chain of military depots set up to subdue the Highlanders; since 1876 the buildings have been converted into a Benedictine abbey. One of the monks of Fort Augustus, Dom Cyril Dieckhoff, was an ardent monster-watcher. It was he who recorded first-hand accounts of monster sightings in Loch Shiel and Loch Morar. From the southern shore of Loch Ness you can see its only island, about 150 yards offshore. In fact it is an artifical island, or crannog, dating from prehistoric times when the safest house was one surrounded by water. Crannogs are still to be found in many lochs, and some were inhabited at least until the 16th century. Fort Augustus, a busy village, also has an exhibition centre. The piers you see rising from the river once carried a railway line that ran from here down to join the West Highland Railway near Fort William; you can also see the locks of the Caledonian Canal (opened 1847), which enables smaller vessels to sail through the Great Glen from the North Sea to the Atlantic coast.

Continuing south along the A82 past Invergarry, you come to a monument by the roadside, the "Well of the Heads", a reminder of gory deeds in the clan warfare of the 16th century. On the left is Loch Oich, smallest and shallowest of the Great Glen lochs; the road then veers to the east side of the glen to rise above Loch Lochy (540 feet deep). At Spean Bridge, if time allows, turn right on to the B8004 for Gairlochy, where the canal enters Loch Lochy, and turn right again to follow the B8005 by Bunarkaig and Clunes to the foot of Loch Arkaig. Here you are in Cameron country, and Achnacarry, seat of Cameron of Lochiel (see Prince Charlie Trail) is close to here. It was of Loch Arkaig that the Earl of Malmesbury, who owned much of the land around it, wrote in 1857:

> …*my stalker and his boy gave me an account of a mysterious creature, which they say exists in Loch Arkaig, and which they call the Lake-horse….My stalker has seen it twice, and both times at sunrise in summer on a bright sunny day, when there was not a ripple on the water. The creature was basking on the surface; he only saw the head and hindquarters, proving that its back was hollow, which is not the shape of any fish or of a seal.*

It is tempting to follow this remote and beautiful loch further, but the Trail turns back to Gairlochy, where you follow the B8004 towards Banavie and **Fort William**. This way, you are looking straight towards the humped massif of Ben Nevis, highest mountain in the British Isles (4406 ft/1535m), though its stupendous south-facing cliffs are hidden from view. Fort William, whose military fortress is now occupied by a public park, is a busy centre of trade and tourism, with an excellent museum.

The trail swings westwards at Banavie on to the A830, the "Road to the Isles". With the sea-fiord of Loch Eil to the left, you drive 10 miles to **Glenfinnan**. The head of Loch Shiel

Fort William with Ben Nevis behind, viewed across Loch Linnhe from Stronchreggan

is very close to the road, at the site of the monument to 1745, but the rivers converging here make it difficult to walk the shore for very far. To see more of it, you turn left off the A830 about a mile before Glenfinnan, just after passing under the railway bridge, and cross the River Callop. From here a track runs to the right, following the course of the stream, then bending leftwards below the woods to emerge on the side of the loch, with a fine view across to Beinn Odhar Mhor ("Big Brown Hill", 2,497ft/870m) and Beinn Odhar Bheag ("Little Brown Hill"), which is actually higher at 2,531ft/882m. Loch Shiel is a freshwater loch, 16 miles long and over 300 feet deep. Monster sightings were recorded here in 1874, 1905 and 1926. 'Shiela' was said to have three humps.

Back on the A830, you follow it west towards Mallaig as far as **Morar** (24 miles). The road is a switchback with some single-track sections (passing places are used) and superb views on all sides, including seawards to the isles of Eigg and Rum. (This section of the trail is also part of the "Prince Charlie" Trail.) Two miles on from Morar is Mallaig, terminus of road and railway, and a ferry-port for South Skye and the Inner Hebrides. To reach Loch Morar, alleged haunt of "Morag", turn right for Morar village and go over the level crossing towards Bracora.

Loch Morar fills one of the deepest hollows in Europe, plunging over 1,000 feet below sea level. The River Morar, on the west side and falling 40 feet to the sea, is one of the world's shortest rivers. The western end of the loch is studded with islands. From Bracora, a track extends along the north shore, worth following both for the views and the sense of peace. When sighted in 1947, the Morar monster was described as being 30 feet long, with four humps, rising about 2 feet above the level of the water. Following another sighting in 1969, a "Loch Morar Survey" was begun in 1970. But Loch Morar has never been explored as intensively as Loch Ness; its surface, with that astounding depth below, is even more enigmatic. And there we leave the monsters of Scotland.

For your return along the A830, refer to the Prince Charlie Trail to explore other aspects of this fascinating area. If returning to Inverness, try the road along the east side of Loch Ness: turn right at Fort Augustus on to the B862, which climbs inland, and then after 9 miles go left on the B852 which swings back to the loch-side with fine views of the loch and also fine waterfall scenery at Foyers (3 miles), and forest walks and a visitor centre at Inverfarigaig (3 miles). Between Foyers and Inverfarigaig is a network of pathways through delightful forest and crag scenery; it is well worth exploring this if your time allows. Follow the B862 into Inverness (18 miles). This route follows narrower roads but carries far less traffic – it has a more "Highland" feel about it.

TRAIL 9

Heartland of the Picts: In Search of a Lost People

Eastern Scotland from St Andrews to Brechin. Two days, from Edinburgh

This trail begins at St Andrews, about an hour and a half's drive from Edinburgh, taking the A90 over the Forth Road Bridge, then the M90 to Junction 8, and from there the A91 via Auchtermuchty and Cupar to St Andrews (62 miles). Alternatively you can go via the "East Neuk" of Fife (see Trail of the Silver Darlings).

St Andrews, a university town since 1411, was the country's ecclesiastical capital from the 10th century to the Reformation (1560), and since the 19th century has been the world headquarters of golf, a game introduced to the world from Scotland. You may well want to explore other aspects of this small but many-faceted town. But this trail homes in on one of its greatest treasures, a relic of that enigmatic people, the Picts – the "St Andrews Sarcophagus".

The Scots (see Campbell's Kingdom Trail) only began to colonise the country in the 6th century. But "Scotland" had already been inhabited, for thousands of years. The first speakers of Celtic languages to reach it came during the first millennium BC, the last ripple of a great folk-movement that had begun long before and far away beyond the Black Sea. They had iron weapons, and imposed themselves as rulers on the peoples already living in the country.

By the time the Romans arrived in AD 79, a tribal society had evolved that included both the original inhabitants and the Celtic speakers. Around 143, the Romans completed a short-lived northern frontier wall between the Firths of Forth and Clyde: the Antonine Wall. The tribes to the north of this they called Caledonians; those who lived near it, the Maeatae. These names are based on the tribes' own names. From the late 3rd century, the word Picti is found in Latin for the northern tribes. This word was for long assumed to mean "painted people", and fantastic visions of tattooed naked Picts were drawn. But this name too may be from the people's own name for themselves. Not much is known of the Picts; remarkably little for a people who dominated a large part of the country for seven hundred years.

The reason for this can be summed up in two words: the Scots. From their first bases in Argyll, these 5th and 6th century immigrants from Ireland spread eastwards and north-wards. Although they and the Picts both spoke Celtic languages, they were not of the same branch. The Scots' language, Gaelic, which was also the language of the new religion, Christianity, became the national one. Picts and Scots co-existed, sometimes amicably, often at war. In the fashion of royal families, their rulers sometimes inter-married, with the result that the Picts sometimes had a king who had been born a Scot, and vice versa. Picts and Scots also fought with or against other neighbours, the Britons of the south-west, and the recently-arrived Anglians of the south-east. Through the 6th, 7th and 8th centuries, a tortuous series of wars and alliances can be pieced together. In 839 Kenneth, son of Alpin, and by tradition son of a Pictish mother, became King of the Scots. Five years later he also became King of the Picts. From then on, Picts and Scots were united in a single nation. It was the language, the customs and institutions of the Scots which survived in the new kingdom, eclipsing the culture of the Picts, though the two traditions took several generations to fuse together. The Picts had been there first, and were probably more numerous, but the new identity was Scotland. Nevertheless we can be sure that Pictish genes are plentiful in the genetic make-up of today's Scots.

What we know of the Picts is pieced together from other peoples' records, from certain place-names, from archaeological finds, and above all from the only tangible evidence they have left, their stone carvings. The cathedral of St Andrews was a priory church, served by Augustinian canons; in the restored "warming room" of their monastery is a collec-tion of carved stones and other items, with the prime one being the sarcophagus, or "tomb-shrine". This has been dated to around AD 825, and may have been made for the Pictish King Constantine. It shows a strongly modelled figure of David with his harp, a favourite subject of classic Pictish sculpture, together with a pastoral and hunting scene; the side panels have finely executed interlace and mesh-work. This has been

Pictish stone cross, Aberlemno, Angus

described as "one of the outstanding examples of Dark Age art to be found in Europe." Entry into the cathedral ruins is free; there is an admission charge for the museum. There is also a good town museum in Kinburn Park, at the opposite, western, end of the town.

St Andrews Cathedral Visitor Centre and Museum, *St Andrews, Fife; tel 01334 472563* (open daily April–Sept, 9.30am–6.30pm; Oct–March, Mon–Sat 9.30am–4.30pm; Sun 2pm–4.30pm).

St Andrews Museum, *Kinburn Park, St Andrews, Fife; tel 01334 412690* (open Nov–Feb, daily, 10am–5pm; March–June and Sept–Oct, daily, 10am–6pm; July–Aug, daily, 9am–7pm).

You may well want to add some time to your tour to see more of St Andrews, whose name and rise to fame shows that power politics was a game already played by Picts and Scots. It was a Pictish area, and the legend of the apostle Andrew's bones having been brought here from Greece was fostered by Oengus,

King of the Picts. At that time the Vikings had overrun Iona, the original centre of the Scots' Church, and the Scots had moved their religious headquarters to **Dunkeld**. The St Andrew story enabled the small monastery here to become a great pilgrim centre, and by the 10th century its prestige made it the main centre of the Church.

The trail leads on towards the heartland of the Picts. Leave St Andrews on the A91 as far as Cupar (10 miles), where you branch right on to the A913, past Newburgh (it was new in the 12th century) to Abernethy (4 miles). As you travel along, look out for another relic of the Picts – found in place-names of farms, hamlets and some villages. Names beginning with Pit- reflect a one-time Pictish settlement. The word, not found in Scottish Gaelic, was originally *pett*, and meant a parcel or share of land. It is found only in eastern and northern Scotland.

Abernethy was an important site in Pictland, for some time the centre of the Pictish Church, and a royal residence. The village centre retains one of the two round towers in Scotland that date from the 10th century or earlier. Rising by the main square with its old market cross, it is 74 feet high, and tapers from a base of 48 feet to 32 feet at the top. Probably built as a refuge, it also has a definite monumental quality. Whoever built this tower were proud to display their culture and skill. The Gaelic name of these towers means "bell-house",

St Andrews, Fife, with the ruins of the Cathedral in the foreground

probably referring to the consecrated handbells which the monks would bring into the place of refuge, along with other treasures, when threatened by a raid from the sea-borne Vikings. Whether for use or as a grim decoration, there is a set of 'jougs', a collar for restraining ill-doers, fixed into the lower wall.

Continue on the A913 for about a mile and fork right on to the A912, signed to Perth. At Bridge of Earn turn left on to the B935 which in about 4 miles leads you to the tiny village of Forteviot. The site is a strategic one, on the southern slope of Strathearn, protected to the west by the Water of May. Earn may be the same word as Erin, a name bestowed by the Scots in memory of their Irish homeland as they encroached eastwards into the Pictish kingdom. Close by the church is Holy Hill, where the Pictish kings had a fortress. It was a favourite place of Kenneth MacAlpin and retained its importance into the time of Duncan, Macbeth and Malcolm Canmore. But as Dunfermline was preferred by Malcolm, Forteviot fell into complete ruin, and what might have been a capital city is a crossroads hamlet.

Follow the B934 across the railway and river to join the A9, and turn right for **Perth** (6 miles). Cross the town following signs for the A93 Blairgowrie and the A94 Coupar Angus; turn left after the bridge over the Tay, then right for the A94. This road takes you into Strathmore (the "great wide valley"), a continuation of the fertile Strathearn. You can see why the Picts treasured this green region, and why the Scots wanted to push in from their bare mountains to the west.

Eighteen miles from Perth is Meigle, with a rich crop of Pictish sculpture housed in its museum. For many centuries, the Pictish sculptures were treated casually or even with contempt. Many have been lost. Others have been incorporated into local buildings, often as lintels or window-sills. Others have simply weathered away. Conservationists are torn between preserving them on-site or housing them in a weatherproof museum, where part of their "magic" is lost. Currently there is a trend to house the finest examples, but to leave identical replicas, formed from resin, on the original site.

Meigle Sculptured Stone Museum, *near Coupar Angus, Perthshire; tel 01828 640 612* (open April–Sept, Mon–Sat 9.30am–6.30pm, Sun 2.00pm–6.30pm).

Of the 30-plus stones from the Meigle area, 25 are kept here. It is an excellent place to get a feel for Pictish sculpture and its three different phases, sometimes defined as Class I, Class II and Class III. Class I stones are the oldest (up to the 8th century), usually cut into the natural stone. Class II shows a change to using a prepared level surface, at first with designs chiselled into it, later with the designs standing out from it – by this time, there is Christian symbolism included in the designs. Nechtan, an early 8th-century Pictish king, became a Christian, and Class II stones are believed to date from his time. The youngest stones are of Class III, where the Pictish symbols are no longer used, and these are assumed to have been carved after the union of the Picts and Scots, from around AD 850. The display is dominated by a great upright cross-slab which, as even an academic art historian said, "seems to vibrate" with life, such is the clarity and intensity of the work. It is only in the past hundred years that the unique quality of these carvings has become appreciated and raised interest in the people who could produce such work. Their world of warriors, animals, monsters and strange symbols seems as far from ours as the Hittite carvings in the Middle East.

Three miles further along the A94, take the short loop on the left via Eassie churchyard. In among the graves is a fine Class II cross-slab, 6ft 8ins high, carved on both front and back. In another mile you come to Glamis. In the garden of the Manse (minister's house) by the church is "King Malcolm's Stone", 8ft 9ins high. This stone is of particular interest for two reasons: one side appears to be early Class I carving; the other is the later Class II, suggesting some respect on the part of the later sculptor for his predecessor's work. On this side, the designs are partly in relief (raised from the surface) and partly incised (cut into the surface), suggesting they were done at a time of change from the incised to the relief style. Fragments of other stones are in the church vestibule, and another stone can be seen a little way along the A94, on the left-hand side, at Hunter's Hill.

Glamis has non-Pictish attractions also: an attractive old-world village street; Glamis Castle (seat of the Earls of Strathmore) with its 14th-century keep; and, at the other end of the social scale, the attractive Angus Folk Museum, housed in a set of 19th-century cottages.

Follow the A94 into the town of Forfar (6 miles), exiting on the B9128 signed for Carnoustie, but turn off after about 2 miles on the minor road to the left signed for Dunnichen. Here, just to the east of the village at its crossroads, was fought the crucial battle of Nechtansmere in AD 685, when the Picts routed the invading Angles from Northumbria, killed their king, Ecgfrith, drove the invaders south across the Firth of Forth, and ensured the survival of their own kingdom. Dunnichen means "Nechtan's Fort", and Nechtan was the name of several Pictish kings. The fort itself disappeared when the hill above "Nechtan's Mere" was quarried in the 19th century, but by the modern cairn, set up on the 1300th anniversary of the battle, is a cast of the Dunnichen Stone, a Class I stone from the 7th century, probably pre-dating the battle. The original is in the museum at Forfar.

Meffan Institute, *20 West High Street, Forfar, Angus; tel 01307 464123* (open all year, Mon–Sat 10am–5pm).

From Dunnichen, follow the minor road eastwards across the A932, past Balgavies, over the B9113, past Turin ("little hill") to Aberlemno. In the churchyard is a fine Pictish cross, whose interlace pattern is the most complex of any known Pictish carving. There are also other stones, whose carved warriors are believed to commemorate the battle fought at Nechtansmere. Not far off, opposite the village hall, are three further stones in a walled enclosure. The cross, with its mourning angels, seems to foreshadow medieval art. It stands on its original site – the other two have been placed here in modern times.

An interesting short walk can be made up Turin Hill. The road to the hill branches to the left off the B8134 a mile west of Aberlemno. It rises through a strip of woodland. Park by the roadside and walk the short, though quite steep, track up to the hill (about 15 minutes each way). At 723ft/252m it is not a high hill, but it does give you an excellent impression of the countryside, though the present-day field pattern and planned woodland is nothing like the wilder woods and little strip-fields of Pictish times. The earthworks on the hill are the remains of a prehistoric camp, built by people who preceded the Picts.

From Aberlemno, follow the unclassified road south past a right-hand and a left-hand junction to Turin, crossing the B9113, and turning left on to the A932 (5 miles). Follow this road to Friockheim (the German -heim was added by an 18th-century landowner to show he had been there) and turn right on to the A933 signed to Arbroath. At the outskirts of Arbroath you pass an airfield to the left; at the end of this, take the unclassified road to the left, signed for St Vigeans. Now a suburb, this community's name commemorates the Irish St Fechan, who died in AD 644. This was another district rich in carved stones, mostly sited around the ancient church which was replaced by the present 19th-century one. Around thirty, from whole stones to fragments, are preserved in the little cottage museum.

St Vigeans Museum, St Vigeans, near Arbroath, Angus; tel 01241 873858 (open April–Sept, Mon–Sat 9.30am–6.30pm, Sun 2pm–6.30pm. Outside April–Sept, telephone to arrange admittance).

Although you have now passed through the "heartland" of the Picts, you have only covered a small extent of their territory, which stretched north of here as far as the Shetland Islands, before the Vikings claimed them in the 9th century. From St Vigeans, return to the A933 and turn right to head for Brechin (15 miles). This is one of the little ancient cathedral-cities of which Scotland has numerous examples, from **Kirkwall** in Orkney to Dunblane in Perthshire. Adjoining the cathedral here is Scotland's other round tower, at 87 feet taller than Abernethy's, and narrower, with a doorway 6 feet above present ground level. The cathedral was founded in 1150, and most of the ancient remains date from the 13th century. But before the bishopric was established, there was a religious community here (as at St Andrews and other places), an abbey of the Culdees ("servants of God"), a peculiarly Celtic religious order who took no formal vows and were allowed to marry and hold property (though the wives had to live outside the abbey). The Culdees disappeared in the 12th century when the Benedictine and other monastic orders were brought in from Europe.

Although there is not much Pictish material in the town, Brechin offers the "experience" of Pictavia in the country park that surrounds the modernised castle (in whose hall King John Balliol of Scotland was forcibly deposed by

Edward I of England, in 1296). Though some elements of the show are imaginary, it gives you a lively introduction to the world of the Picts as revealed by their carving and jewellery.

Pictavia, *Brechin, Angus; tel 01307 461460 (www.pictavia.org)* (open June–August, Mon–Sat 9am–6pm, Sun 10am–6pm; Sept–May, Mon–Sat 9am–5pm, Sun 10am–5pm).

Among other items of non-Pictish interest, Brechin is home of a preserved steam railway, that runs from the old railway station to nearby Bridge of Dun, and has many steam-age artefacts on show. From here, return to Edinburgh via the A935, signed for Forfar; this joins the A90 a mile outside the town; follow the A90 to Dundee and the Tay Road Bridge (27 miles), then the A92 the rest of the way to the M90, where you bear left for the southbound carriageway heading to the Forth Road Bridge and Edinburgh (56 miles).

TRAIL 10

The Monks of Melrose, and Sir Walter Scott

One day, from Edinburgh

If you would view fair Melrose aright,
Go visit it by pale moonlight…

So wrote Sir Walter Scott, at the height of the era of Romantic writing, when people were less interested in the detail and history of ruined abbeys than in the pleasantly eerie sensation they got when looking through ruined arches at flying clouds and a ghostly moon. But if you choose to stay the night in Melrose, you can test out Sir Walter's assertion.

The right place for this trail to begin is in East Princes Street Gardens, Edinburgh, where the Scott Monument rises in lofty pinnacles above the writer's statue. Scott was bred to be a lawyer, and indeed was Sheriff of Roxburghshire. But his fame rests on his dual literary career: first as a writer of long narrative poems, beginning with *The Lay of the Last Minstrel* in 1805; then, when these went out of fashion, he virtually invented the historical novel, and wrote such famed books as *Waverley*, *Ivanhoe*, *Rob Roy* and many others. For a time he was the most widely read author in the world. He made, lost and remade a fortune. For most people in his day, he was "Mr Scotland" and he is very much the godfather of all the tartan-and-clanship imagery that not only bedecks the Scottish tourist trade but still affects the modern Scottish soul. The humour, action and story-telling of Scott's novels keeps almost all of them in print, even though his relaxed and rambling style takes some getting used to.

The Monument itself was put up in 1840–44, and designed by George Kemp, who was a great admirer of Melrose Abbey and followed its Gothic style in these soaring pointed arches. The inner staircase rises 200 feet (no lift) and gives a fine view of central Edinburgh from the upper stages. Niches contain statues representing some of Scott's best-known characters. Of Scotland's two most famous writers, in Edinburgh it is Scott who dominates. Scott and Burns met only once, in an

The Scott Monument, Princes Street, Edinburgh

Edinburgh drawing-room in 1786, when Scott was a boy of 15.

The Scott Monument, *Princes Street, Edinburgh; tel 0131 529 4068 (open all year, Mon–Sat 9.30am–6pm).*

From Edinburgh, leave following signs for the A7 and Galashiels, and follow this road all the way (32 miles); continue through the town to the south end and turn left at the roundabout on to the A6091 for Melrose, then after crossing the river turn right on to the B6360, and you will see signs for Abbotsford (two and a half miles). Follow these to this house by the River Tweed where Scott lived for the last 21 years of his life.

He bought the site, then called "Clarty Hole" ("muddy place"), in 1811 and had this many-turreted house built (the west wing is the earliest part), giving it the more dignified name of "Abbotsford". Somewhat squeezed in between road and river, the house is full of memorabilia of Sir Walter, especially in his library, the armoury and the study. But it is also remarkable for all the artefacts eagerly collected by Scott during his life. He was an inveterate picker-up of curiosities and his home is a museum to his jackdaw tastes. Among its many items are: Rob Roy MacGregor's sporran, sword and dirk; a quaich (broad cup) from which Prince Charlie drank; and the keys of Lochleven Castle (see Mary, Queen of Scots Trail). The whole effect is somewhat overpowering. A 20th-century Scottish poet, Edwin Muir, called Abbotsford "this pompous, crude, fantastic, unmanageable, heartless, insatiable, comfortless brute of a house". Look out for the portrait of Scott in the "Chinese Drawing Room"; this, by Sir Henry Raeburn, gives a sense of the energy and passion that produced so many millions of words, and the fierce pride that made Scott drive himself to pay off the vast debts incurred by the bankruptcy of his publishing business.

Whatever one's view of the house, Abbotsford is placed on a beautiful stretch of the River Tweed, and many of the trees here were originally planted by Sir Walter Scott. **Abbotsford House**, *near Melrose, Roxburghshire; tel 01896 752043* (open mid March–Oct, Mon–Sat 10am–5pm, Sun 2pm–5pm; June–Aug, Sun 10am–5pm).

From Abbotsford, return on the B6360 to the A6091 and turn right for Melrose (2 miles). Turn off to the left and follow the signs into the small town. The abbey is just off the centre, with a large car park adjacent to it. In the 12th and 13th centuries, which were largely a time of prosperity for Scotland, many priories and abbeys were founded. The sons of King Malcolm III and Queen Margaret were pious men and, as kings, endowed much wealth on new abbeys. They were concerned to bring the new monastic orders into Scotland, to replace the old, informal

Melrose Abbey, Melrose, Borders

Celtic abbeys of the "Culdees". King David I was the most pro-lific founder. In the Border region, the combination of good farmland and rivers rich in fish created wealth which was reflected by the number of abbeys. Within a few miles of Melrose were other great abbeys at Dryburgh, Kelso and Jedburgh.

The first church here was established by the Celtic St Aidan, with monks from Iona, in the 7th century. In 1136, King David invited Cistercian monks from Rievaulx, in north-ern England, to set up a new community here, and he made sure it was generously provided with lands and money. One of the first abbots was his stepson Waldef, later canonised. This royal start ensured that Melrose was always one of the greatest of Scottish abbeys. But when the centuries of warfare between Scotland and England began, Melrose and the other Border abbeys were vulnerable. English invaders were no respecters of religious houses. Three times Melrose was destroyed in the 14th century; a largely new church was built in the 15th cen-tury but this was heavily damaged in the English invasion of 1545. Fifteen years later, the revolutionary events of the Reformation ensured that the battered monastery would never be rebuilt.

The Cistercians chose their sites for their isolation and natural beauty; Melrose is no longer isolated but its setting is splendid. The original architecture was plain and severe, but the 15th-century rebuild was undertaken when the most flam-boyant period of Gothic architecture was beginning. Especially in the British Isles, this was the era of perpendicular building, with wide, soaring windows and intervening wall-spaces richly carved and decorated. The opulence of the Melrose ruins has an un-Scottish feel about it, which adds to its interest. The masons who designed it came from England and perhaps also France, but many of the mason-carvers were Scots, as the curly kale leaves carved in capitals and bosses suggest (not to mention the bagpipe-playing pig who leans out from the south side at roof level).

The Cistercians began as an austere order of monks divided into professed monks, who maintained the religious ritual, and "lay brothers" who did the agricultural and manu-al work of the monastery, which owned large tracts of farmland and forest. Melrose had two hundred lay brothers, which explains the large scale of the monastic buildings to the north of the church. The layout of these is clear, and helpful information boards indicate the function and original appearance of the buildings. At the entrance to the abbey is also a small museum which preserves some of the finer carving that has been found on the site. Of the carved and gilded wooden ornamentation and furniture, the gold crucifixes and the stained glass, nothing remains. Even before the Scots turned Protestant and smashed all the "idols", relics and statues of their churches, the greed of rich landowners, appointed as "commendators" supposedly for the protection of the abbeys, brought about the disappearance of much of their portable wealth. In Melrose it is possible to reflect what Scotland might have been like if John Knox and his colleagues had failed to get the population on their side. But long before 1560, the Church had gone rotten – the Cistercians had forgotten their vows of poverty. Reform was overdue, but when it came, it came with a vengeance.

Quite a lot of the fabric of the church, and most of that of the abbey buildings that surrounded it, is now to be found in the stone buildings of Melrose town. From the 1560s on, the abandoned abbey was treated as a quarry. The ugly roof that covers the three easternmost bays of the nave was put up in the 17th century, when this part was used as a parish church; it replaced the far more elegant rib vaults that local masons no longer had the skill to construct, nor the church elders the money to pay for.

King Alexander II of Scotland is said to be buried here, but no king, apart from David I, is more closely associated with Melrose than Robert I, "the Bruce". He provided the then very large sum of £2,000 to assist rebuilding after the English army had wrecked the place. He also asked that his heart should be buried here after his death (first it was taken on a crusade to Spain, and retrieved from a disastrous rout of the Scots crusaders). In 1921 a mummified heart sealed in a lead casket was found in the abbey ruins, and has been re-interred in the chapter house, where it had been discovered.

Melrose Abbey, *Melrose; tel 01896 822562* (open April–Sept, Mon–Sat 9.30am–7pm, Sun 2pm–7pm; Oct–March, Mon–Sat 9.30am–4pm, Sun 2pm–4pm).

From Melrose, take the A6091 out of the town, turning right

"Scott's View" – the River Tweed and the Eildon Hills

on to the A68 at Newtown St Boswells, and follow the A68 into St Boswells (4 miles). For real Scott fans, this road passes by Dryburgh Abbey, where Sir Walter is buried.

Dryburgh Abbey, *near St Boswells, tel 01835 822381* (open April–Sept, Mon–Sat 9.30am–7pm, Sun 2pm–7pm; Oct–March, Mon–Sat 9.30am–4pm, Sun 2pm–4pm).

You are on your way to share an experience in which Scott revelled during his lifetime. In St Boswells, turn left on to the B6404, and follow this road for a mile to Clintmains, where you turn left on to the B6356, signed for Bemersyde and Earlston. The way bends back along the north bank of the Tweed, and about 2 miles along is "Scott's View", the great man's favourite sight in all Scotland. You are looking across the valley towards the miniature mountains of the Eildon Hills, whose shapes have a strangely captivating air. The Romans built a camp near here and called the hills Trimontium, "triple hills". Later legends say that the hills were split apart by the Devil, at the order of Michael Scott, a celebrated local wizard of medieval times. According to another story, the kingdom of Fairyland lies beneath these hills, and it was to here that the poet "Thomas the Rhymer", in a famous Scots ballad, was transported for seven years by the Queen of the Fairies:

True Thomas lay on Huntlie bank,
A ferlie he spied wi' his e'e;
And there he saw a lady bright
Come riding down by the Eildon Tree.

Continue north on the B6356 to Earlston, and turn right on to the A68, signposted for Edinburgh. This route takes you back to Edinburgh (33 miles) through the attractive, old-fashioned little town of Lauder.

TRAIL 11

Glasgow's River: The Clyde Trail

One day, from Glasgow

The name of the River Clyde is a reminder of the Britons, whose kingdom of Strathclyde stretched from north of Glasgow down into Cumbria in England, until it was merged into Scotland in 1032. Their language was similar to Old Welsh, and the name "Clyde", like Welsh Clwyd, means "cleansing stream".

The town of Glasgow was placed north of the river, and although it has now spread vastly on both sides, it has not placed its monumental buildings right by the river, as London and Paris have. In recent years, however, the riverfront has been spruced up and some major new developments have been situated on it.

The trail begins to the east of the city centre, by the footbridge across the Clyde, linking the sites of Glasgow's shiny new Science Exhibition Centre and the Scottish Exhibition and Conference Centre. The Science Centre is a multi-million

The People's Palace, Glasgow Green, Glasgow

pound "Millennium" project, due to open in 2001; its architecture a reminder that this, the city of Charles Rennie Mackintosh, prides itself on its finest buildings (there are many not so fine). Below this point, the river is hemmed by shipyard and industrial sites, but upstream, you can follow the quays on the north bank towards the city centre. As the name suggests, these were once places where ships tied up; the Broomielaw was famous as the embarkation point for steamer trips down the river and out into the Firth of Clyde. The last of the Clyde paddle steamers, *Waverley*, still does trips from Anderston Quay during June–August (tel 0141 287 4017).

Seven bridges cross the river in the central part, carrying roads, railways and a footpath. Across the river from Clyde Street is the Gorbals district, once notorious as a slum area. At the end of Clyde Street you reach Glasgow Green. This area of parkland by the river has always been one of the city's lungs, most valuable in its industrial heyday. Among the pathways is set the "People's Palace", established in 1898 as a museum of the city's history (admission free).

The People's Palace, *Glasgow Green, Glasgow; tel 0141 554 0223* (open all year, daily except Tues, 10am–5pm).

From Glasgow Green the river winds away through an urban and suburban setting. You will meet it again at Uddingston, in a very different setting. Leave the city on the M74, signed for Carlisle, and come off at Junction 3 (1 mile); turn left at the first roundabout and right at the second, on to the A74 Glasgow Road and follow this under a trio of motorway bridges to where the road divides, with the A721 branching left. You follow Glasgow Road to the right into Uddingston, past the railway station to Main Street and the central square, where you turn right into Castle Avenue, and follow this road until you see the sign for Bothwell Castle, on the right-hand side (about one and a half miles), and its car park.

Here we see the river as a protective barrier. On a rocky outcrop above the stream stands the still-massive ruin of a castle built in the mid 13th century. Its main feature is the circular keep – an innovation in its time – rising 90 feet high, with walls 15 feet thick. Bothwell Castle played an important part in the early 14th-century Wars of Independence. It was built by the de Moravia, or Murray, family. In 1298 it was taken by the English, and besieged for a time by William Wallace. The site made Bothwell a strong point, and the river also eased its communications. (That small ships and boats used the river we know because a little way downstream is the town of Cambuslang, whose name means "beaching place of the ships"). The castle now stands in pleasant wooded parkland.

Bothwell Castle, *Castle Avenue, Uddingston, Lanarkshire; tel 01698 816894* (open daily April–Sept, Mon–Sat 9.30am–7pm, Sun 2pm–7pm).

Continue down Castle Avenue and turn right into Blantyre Road (1 mile), then in a few yards, right again into Blantyre Mill Road. From here you can cross the river by a footbridge and walk up to the David Livingstone Centre. This was the birthplace (1813) and boyhood home of Scotland's most famous explorer, first European discoverer of the Victoria Falls in Africa, and a tireless campaigner against the African slave trade. Before studying to become a doctor, Livingstone worked as a child-labourer in the textile mills here. Although the building looks imposing, it was in fact a tenement block and the large Livingstone family occupied one room, which is preserved. The rest of the museum is dedicated to Livingstone's life and explorations in Africa.

David Livingstone Centre, *165 Station Road, Blantyre, Lanarkshire; tel 0141 332 7133* (26 May–23 Dec, Mon–Sat 10am–5pm, Sun 12.30pm–5pm).

Returning to your car, follow Blantyre Mill Road back until you turn right into Main Street in the town of Bothwell (about three quarters of a mile). About a mile further on, the road (B7071) crosses the Clyde at Bothwell Bridge. A monument on the left, just before the bridge, recalls that here on 22 June 1679, during the bitter religious wars of the period, the Battle of Bothwell Brig was fought between an army of Presbyterian "Covenanters" and the Royal Dragoons commanded by the Duke of Monmouth. The over-confident Covenanters were routed.

Follow Bellshill Road (B7071) to the left of the monument and on to Junction 5 of the M74 (half a mile). Join the motorway southbound for Carlisle, and leave it at Junction 7

(6 miles), on the A72 signed for **Lanark**, following an attractive, placid, wooded reach of the Clyde for 11 miles. In the centre of the small town of Lanark, look for signs to New Lanark, branching off from the upper end of High Street, via Wellgate and Braxfield Road. The road twists down into the river valley. From the car park, steps lead down towards the settlement of New Lanark (2 miles). It is possible to drive right down, though this is officially restricted to business visitors and residents, and you may find it difficult to get a parking space.

Here we have the river contributing its water-power as an aid to industry. The mills down here, using a system of mill-streams drawn off the river, were built in 1784. It was intended to be an ideal working community, with good housing for the workers, opportunities for leisure and cultivation, schools for the children and – for the time – decent working conditions. New Lanark set new standards, and many people came to view the "experiment"; the whole place is remarkably well conserved. Nevertheless, it must be said that some of the buildings, so tall, so grey, so hemmed in by the steep banks, have a somewhat jail-like appearance. A number of the buildings are museum-spaces, others are commercial centres. There is a "millennium ride" through time, focused around a young girl-worker's own experience. The girl, Annie McLeod, who died in 1820, appeared opportunely as a ghost in the 1990s. An early visitor, the social commentator William Cobbett watched a dancing-class in the schoolroom, the boys dressed in kilts, the girls in short dresses, and speculated sardonically on the pre-marital birth-rate.

New Lanark, *tel 01555 665876* (open daily throughout the year, 11am–5pm).

Walking upstream from New Lanark, you see the source of the water-power. The Clyde here tumbles over the rocks in a series of falls, in what hydrographers refer to as an "adjustment" of its course. This area is a Nature Reserve, with badger setts and peregrine falcon nests, and we see the river both as an element in the ecology of the region and as a place of scenic beauty. A good footpath leads up to Corra Linn (2 miles; about an hour and a half for the round walk). Above the path the crumbling "Wallace Tower" (connections with the hero unproven) adds a dramatic element to the scene. Corra Linn itself ("round pool") is a deep, dark pool at the bottom of an 86-foot series of cascades over great shelves of granitic rock. This has long been a favourite walking place for dwellers in the Clyde Valley. Modern industry has harnessed the water for hydro-electric power, and the full force of the stream is sent over the Falls only on certain days.

Here is where the trail ends, though the path and the river go on. The river flows round Lanark in a great bend, for some distance actually flowing southwards. We are about 25 miles away in a straight line from its headwaters in the Lowther Hills (scene of the Lead Miners' Trail), but the meanderings of the river's course almost double this. Out of the green farmlands the valley gradually rises to cut through grassy hillsides and then brown mountain slopes, before the point where the swift-flowing Daer Burn is joined by a cheeky little mountain stream called Clydes Water, which, although smaller, gives its name to the combined river from then on; and, as Clydesdale, to a noble breed of working horse. And as Strathclyde, to a once-flourishing kingdom.

From Lanark, return via the A72, signed for Glasgow, joining the M74 at Junction 7 and following it into the city.

TRAIL 12

The Lead Miners

One day, from Edinburgh or Glasgow

More went on in the bare rolling hills of the Southern Uplands than the traditional cattle-thieving and cross-border raiding of the Border Reivers. Here and there amongst their massive folds of hard Silurian and Ordovician rocks are mineral deposits, which have long been identified and mined. The Romans prospected in these hills for lead to make their water pipes. There was also silver, and tantalising but elusive signs of gold in the hill streams. The Scottish crown is made from Leadhills gold. Up in the Lowther Hills, the highest village in Scotland was established as a community of miners.

This trail can be readily combined with the Glasgow's River Trail. Otherwise, leave Glasgow on the M74 south-bound, or Edinburgh on the A702, signposted for Carlisle, joining the M74 at Abington (Junction 13, 41 miles from Edinburgh, 28 from Glasgow). At Junction 14, turn off on to the A702 and follow this road up the valley of the Upper Clyde for a mile, then turn right on to the B7040, branching off just before Elvanfoot. This road goes up the valley of the Elvan Water. The embankments of a dismantled railway line run higher up the slope. Higher still, on the right-hand side, are old mine workings, their shafts and tunnels blocked up or collapsed. The hills are lined with tracks followed by miners and pack-horses. The mottled effect on the slopes is caused by heather-burning. Small areas are burned at different times to allow the best environment for the grouse, game-birds which live in the hills. Young heather shoots are part of their diet; the mature heather plants give them shelter.

At the aptly-named village of Leadhills (6 miles), set in a sheltered cleft in the hills, there is an obelisk in the church-yard in memory of William Symington, who built the world's first paddle-steamer, *Charlotte Dundas*, in 1801, as well as the grave of one John Taylor, said to have died at 137 years of age. Here you join the B797 leading to Wanlockhead (3 miles), the highest village in the country, at 1,531 feet above sea level. In Scotland, this is an inhospitable height to live at, but economic necessity made the choice for the inhabitants. For centuries this has been a lead-mining area. The mine was licensed by the king and the "royalties" from its sales helped to swell the royal purse, always a meagre one by most European standards. Commercial working has long stopped, and the entire complex of mine-workings and buildings – including Symington's workshop – is now a museum.

Wanlockhead village is formed by short terraces of low, white houses, reaching down to the right, on a road that turns into a hill track. Park at the visitor centre, just by the junction, and inside you will be issued with the "Heritage Trail" guide to the locality. The miners' houses are single-storey cottages dating back to the 18th century; prior to that they would have been thatched. The larger houses are those of the foremen or overseers. Some of the cottages have been preserved as museum-houses. As you walk around, you see little wooden doorways set into the hillside, and the ends of pipes protruding here and there. Dotted about on the green grassy slopes are some of the relics of industry, including a water-powered beam-engine, used to pump out a deep shaft. One of the mine entries has been kept open and visitors can enter the tunnels for a guided tour, with graphic descriptions of the hardships encountered by the miners.

One of the most interesting sights of Wanlockhead is the 18th-century Miners' Library, set up in 1756. Here you get a strong sense of the urge for learning and "self-improvement" among all social classes, that turned Scotland into one of the leaders of the industrial and intellectual revolution of the 18th and early 19th centuries. It was a son of the landowner's factor (land agent) at nearby Leadhills, the jovial poet Allan Ramsay (1686–1758), who set up the very first subscription library in Scotland, in Edinburgh in 1728; this library is now dedicated to him. Outside, down by the stream, is a gold-panning centre. What you find, you keep!

Wanlockhead, Museum of Lead Mining, *Wanlockhead, near Biggar, Lanarkshire; tel 01659 74387* (open daily, April–Oct, 10am–4.30pm).

A narrow-gauge railway operates on a short length of track at Leadhills, on the trackbed of Scotland's highest standard-gauge

Wanlockhead Museum of Lead Mining, Lanarkshire

line (now closed). It runs on public holidays, Saturdays and Sundays (www.uel.ac.uk/pers/1278/rly-pres/tlwr.html). From Wanlockhead, return to Edinburgh or Glasgow; or continue on the B797, winding through the spectacular Mennock Pass for 7 miles to the junction with the A76, where you can turn left for Dumfries and the Border Reivers' Trail (26 miles), or right for Mauchline and the Robert Burns Trail (17 miles).

TRAIL 13

The Border Reivers

Two days, from Edinburgh or Glasgow

Are you descended from a Border family – Armstrongs, Elliots, Grahams, Kerrs, Maxwells, Scotts and many others? If so, perhaps your ancestors were among the Border Reivers: those grim and warlike figures who for hundreds of years profited from the rivalry of Scotland and England to maintain their own lifestyle of raiding and hell-raising.

The main Border families:
Nithsdale and Annandale – The West March: Maxwell, Johnstone, Carlisle, Carruthers.
Liddesdale – The Middle March: Armstrong, Elliot, Nixon.
Teviotdale – The Middle March: Scott, Kerr, Rutherford, Pringle, Tait.
East March: Hume, Dickson.

Robert Burns Centre on the River Nith, Dumfries

This trail can be effectively combined with the Lead Miners Trail.

Leave Glasgow on the M74 southbound, or Edinburgh on the A702, signposted for Carlisle, joining the M74 at Abington (Junction 13, 41 miles from Edinburgh, 28 from Glasgow). If you want to do the Lead Miners Trail, see page 92 at this point.

As an alternative route omitting the lead-mines, and passing through some highly impressive mountain scenery, stay on the A702, following the line of an old Roman military road up the narrow valley of the Patrail Water and through the Lowther Hills via the Dalveen Pass to join the A76, signposted for Dumfries, at Carronbridge (18 miles; 8 miles south of Mennock). Here you are in Nithsdale, with the River Nith winding to your right, at the western edge.

If you have done the Lead Miners Trail, from Wanlockhead, the B797 leads on through the Mennock Pass and winding down the scenic glen of the Mennock Water joins the A76 just south of Mennock (7 miles; turn left for Dumfries).

Travelling down the A76 you are on the edge of what was indeed Scotland's wild west. In the hills to your left, much of them covered by the vast modern Forest of Ae (from the River Ae, meaning "water"), was the homeland of the great Maxwell family.

The border area between England and Scotland, completely separate nations until 1603, was divided into three zones, the East March, the Middle March and West March. Each March had its warden on each side, appointed by the king, and supposed – in times of peace – to work together to maintain law and order. There were special "border laws" which specified how criminals from either side should be dealt with, and provided for "days of truce" when both sides could meet and discuss grievances and problems. During the heyday of the Reivers ("raiders") in the 16th century, this frontier was as lawless and wild as any in the world. The wardens' control was limited at best; often they were among the prime raiders themselves.

Here on the West March, the wardenship was often held by the Maxwells. But the Borderers did not simply raid across the border; there were raids, blood-feuds and dirty deeds among themselves. One of the longest and bloodiest feuds in Scotttish history went on between the Maxwells and the Johnstones, who shared much of the same territory. The Maxwells were more numerous; to achieve dominance, the Johnstones had to try harder.

In the 1580s a virtual war raged across this region, as the head of the Johnstones and Lord Maxwell fought a bitter struggle for power. The king and his advisers could only watch from afar; their power was limited to appointing or dismissing the warden – the office was held, in theory, by a Johnstone. In practice, the Maxwell was out to show that the West March was his preserve.

To your left, south of Ae, in one of the most attractive, "unspoiled" and under-visited farmland areas in the country, is the village of Duncow, one of many places laid waste in this local civil war. A far bigger prize was the town of Dumfries; Johnstone had been appointed its Provost in 1584, but Maxwell barred his entry to the town. Maxwell was outlawed by the king – a last resort – who supplied Johnstone with additional men. But Maxwell found allies among the other "riding families"; with an army of up to 2,000 men he took the war right into Johnstone's territory, raiding the town of Lockerbie, capturing the Johnstone castle of Lochmaben, and finally capturing and imprisoning Johnstone himself. Maxwell set up a gallows in Dumfries and threatened to hang the Warden-Provost from it. The Maxwells had won; in 1585 he was again Warden of the West March. But the feud was to go on for another twenty years.

Dumfries (14 miles; "fort among the thickets") is the regional capital of the old West March, with many historical associations. Here Robert the Bruce murdered his rival, John Comyn, in 1306. Robert Burns is buried here (see below). It was a Maxwell town (there is an actual Maxwelltown just to the west); its present handsome and open aspect is different to the compact old walled town. Its castle stood on the site occupied by Greyfriars Church (not the same church of Bruce's crime), at the upper end of High Street.

If you have done the Robert Burns Trail (see pages 121–7) then there is a tailpiece to it here, as its true end is in Dumfries. In 1788 the poet rented Ellisland Farm outside the town (7 miles north of the town on the A76 Kilmarnock Road, right-hand side, signed). The farmhouse, hardly changed in appearance, has rooms with Burns memorabilia, and access to the poet's walk by the River Nith. It was here that he wrote "Auld Lang Syne", "Tam o' Shanter" and many others of his finest lyrics.

Ellisland Farm, *Holywood Road, Auldgirth, Dumfries; tel 01387 740426* (open April–Sept, Mon–Fri 10am–1pm and 2pm–5pm, Sun 2pm–5pm; Oct–March, Tues–Sat 10am–4pm).

In 1791, when he was appointed an excise officer, Burns moved into the town, first to Bank Street, then to the house in the "Wee Vennel" (now Burns Street). He died here in 1796, and is buried in St Michael's Churchyard. "Don't let the awkward squad fire over my grave," he begged, but his fellow-volunteers in the local militia nevertheless fired three volleys. At first his was a modest grave, but in 1815 the body was moved to the white temple-like structure, with its "ploughman-poet" statue, that stands out in the far corner of the churchyard. On the riverbank facing the town centre, equidistant from the old stone 15th-century bridge and the 19th-century footbridge, is a Burns Centre which features an audio-visual presentation and exhibition. In the street behind and above the Burns Centre is the Dumfries Museum of the town's long and often eventful history.

Robert Burns Centre, *Mill Road, Dumfries; tel 01387 264808* (open April–Sept, Mon–Sat 10am–5pm, Sun 2pm–5pm; Oct–March, Tues–Sat 10am–1pm and 2pm–5pm).

Burns House, *Burns Street, Dumfries; tel 01387 255297* (open April–Sept, Mon–Sat 10am–5pm, Sun 2pm–5pm; Oct–March, Tues–Sat 10am–1pm and 2pm–5pm).

Dumfries and Galloway Museum, *The Observatory, Church Street, Dumfries; tel 01387 253374* (open daily, Mon–Sat 10am–1pm and 2pm–5pm, Sun 2pm–5pm).

Eight miles south of Dumfries on the B725, and close to the sea, stands the triangular moated Caerlaverock Castle, the chief Maxwell stronghold, with their motto "I bid ye fair" above its gateway. From this fortress access to all south-west Scotland could be controlled. Much of the ruin dates from the 14th century. The Italianate Renaissance building inside was put up after the reiving period had come to an end, in the hope that a more peaceful era had arrived, but it was destroyed in the religious warfare that swept this area in the 1640s. There was always something to fight about. On its level shore, looking west to the peak of Criffel and south to the mountains of Cumbria, the castle remains a commanding place even in ruin. It is surrounded by a National Nature Reserve, the largest "wetland" reserve in Britain, rich in bird-life (open all year).

Caerlaverock Castle, *near Dumfries; tel 01387 770244* (open daily April–Sept, 9.30am–6pm; Oct–March, Mon–Sat 9.30am–4pm).

Returning through Dumfries, the Reivers' Trail takes you eastwards on the A709 towards Lochmaben. The castle here was another strategic one. In the Maxwell–Johnstone war it was held by the Johnstones until the Maxwells stormed it in July 1585. Now little of it remains on its peninsular site above the Castle Loch, a mile south of the town on the B7020. Three miles further along the A709 is Lockerbie. In the 16th century this was a Johnstone town, and in two successive attacks in 1585 the Maxwells set much of it ablaze, hanged four men at their doors, and took away many prisoners. The Johnstones got their revenge in 1593 when, in the last set-piece battle of the Border Reivers, they defeated the Maxwells on the banks of the

Hermitage Castle, Roxburghshire

Dryfe Water. Lord Maxwell himself was killed, according to legend, by the wife of Johnstone, her weapon the huge key of Lochmaben Castle. The battle site slopes towards the river to the north-west of the town.

To view this and the Garden of Remembrance that commemorates the destruction of a PanAm jumbo jet above the town in December 1988, take the road signposted to the cemetery, over the M74 bridge. Leaving the cemetery, turn right on to the minor road towards Dryfesdalegate, where you bear left, cross the river and go on to Dryfeholm Farm. The track leading off to the right takes you about half a mile back to the river and a "Bailey" bridge. Just downstream, on your side, is the site of "Maxwell's Thorn", where Lord Maxwell is reputed to have been felled in the battle. After this battle, fought partly by mounted riders, a "Lockerbie lick" became proverbial for a sword-cut by a rider on a foot-soldier.

From Lockerbie, you head east along the B7068, cutting across the edge of the Southern Uplands, great hill spurs separated by river valleys. Now almost completely unpopulated, four hundred years ago the area was well spread with nests of the "riding families". Depopulation began soon after King James VI of Scotland became King of England also, in 1603. No longer could the Border Reivers play off one side against the other (or be used as pawns by the two governments). They were an embarrassment on both sides, and since they would not give up the only way of life they knew, they were ruthlessly attacked by the King's lieutenants from north and south. Many families were encouraged or compelled to remove to Northern Ireland. Their towers and castles were left roofless; their houses relapsed back into the earth. Over a period of a few years, the lawless Borders became the quiet agricultural land that you still see today.

Here you are entering the Middle March, and what used to be the heartland of the wildest bunch of all, Liddesdale, home of the Armstrongs. At the weaving town of Langholm (18 miles) there is an Armstrong Museum at the former Erskine Church.

Clan Armstrong Museum, *Lodge Walk, Castle Holme, Langholm, Dumfries & Galloway; tel 01387 381610* (open April–Oct, Tues–Sun 1.30pm–4.30pm).

From here, follow the signs to the A7 and Carlisle. Over on your left, beyond the river, is Tarras Moss, where the Armstrongs used to hide out from punitive expeditions: "so surrounded by bogges and marshi ground, with thick bushes and shrubbes, that they fear no force or power of England or Scotland", wrote an English warden. Just past Hagg (three and a half miles) turn left on to the minor road that runs parallel to the A7 and the River Esk, and in half a mile, on the left-hand side, look for signs to Gilnockie Tower. Even from outside, on its site above the river, this is a picturesque home for a bandit chief. It was the home of Johnnie Armstrong, perhaps the most notorious of the reivers until his unfortunate meeting with King James V (see below). The tower, with its reiver memorabilia and its Armstrong "Clan Room", can be visited.

Gilnockie Tower, *near Canonbie, Dumfries & Galloway; tel 01387 371 876* (open April–Oct, Mon–Sat, guided tours at 10am and 2.30pm).

Continue on the same road, bearing left across the river, then right for Canonbie (about 2 miles). Here turn left on to the B6357, and follow it up Liddesdale towards Newcastleton.

Fra the thievis of Liddesdale
May the Lord protect us

So wrote a 16th-century Scottish poet. This was the badlands, and no-one came here who was not a friend of the Armstrongs and Elliots, or who did not have a strong force at his back.
    Eight and a half miles from Canonbie, and a half-mile south of Newcastleton (an 18th-century "new" village) is the ruin of Mangerton Tower, on the left bank of the Liddel Water, once a stronghold of the Armstrongs. In 1320, Alexander, the second Lord of Mangerton was killed by Lord Soulis, who held the nearby Hermitage Castle. Armstrong's crime had been in saving Soulis's life in a fight; rather than live in his debt, Soulis invited him to a meal and had him murdered. His memorial stands above the roadside here, on the left, at Milnholm Cross. On the other side of the valley lived Jock o' the Side, of whom it was said "A greater thief did never ride". Just by the cross, a side road runs up for a mile to Ettleton Churchyard; the

church has vanished, but there is a well-preserved array of gravestones and monuments to Armtrongs, Elliots and others through the centuries. Even after the reiving period, the Armstrongs lived dangerous lives: see the obelisk to William Armstrong of Sorbytrees, shot "without challenge or warning" by the Revd Joseph Smith in 1831. From here you get a fine view of Liddesdale.

A mile past Newcastleton, branch left on to the B6399, signed to Hawick. After 3 miles, just by a bridge, turn left at the Hermitage Castle sign, and after another mile the castle itself looms up on the right-hand of the road. Strikingly well-preserved, it looks intact at first, but the structure is roofless and ruinous inside. The huge pointed arch in the curtain wall linking its east and west towers is the most striking feature of the castle, which has a distinctly forbidding aspect. Many legends are associated with it, including the boiling alive of Lord Soulis by his outraged tenants, goaded by his tyranny and suspecting him of witchcraft. In the later days of the reivers, the Captain of Hermitage held the castle for the Keeper of Liddesdale, whose job it was to supervise the region. Built by the great Comyn family in the 13th century and held, ostensibly at least, in the King's name, it was much larger than the usual tower dwelling of a reiver chieftain. In 1566 it was held by the Earl of Bothwell, and Mary, Queen of Scots came here to visit him in a madcap dash from Jedburgh on horseback, when he lay wounded after a scrap with the Elliots. A short path to the right leads to the remains of a 13th-century chapel and a grave, reputed to be that of "Cout of Kielder", a tyrannical local baron who was drowned – a favourite Border method of execution – in the adjacent stream.

Hermitage Castle, *Hermitage, Newcastleton, Roxburghshire; tel 01387 376222* (open daily, April–Sept, 9.30am–6.30pm; Oct–March, Mon–Wed 9.30am–4.30pm, Fri and Sun 2pm–6pm).

Continue on the narrow road up the valley of the Hermitage Water, with the height of Cauldcleuch looming ahead. This road was originally a reivers' track over which cattle were driven. It may have been the one followed by Johnnie Armstrong of Gilnockie, when he rode with fifty followers to meet King James V in the summer of 1530. The king had come to the Borders with an army in order to assert his own control. Your road comes out of the hills to join the A7 road (8 miles); turn right for Hawick. The way runs through another pass among the hills to come down into Teviotdale. At Carlanrig (about 6 miles), the reiver and the king met. Johnnie, also known as Black Jock, was apparently confident of a friendly reception. Perhaps it was all a trick. He and his men were seized and summarily hanged from the trees that grew by the track. The king's comment on the splendidly-dressed Johnnie, "What wants yon knave that a king should have, But the sword of honour and the crown?" is recalled in a famous Border ballad, as is Johnnie's bitter retort:

To seek hot water beneath cauld ice,
Surely it is a great folly –
I have asked grace at a graceless face,
But there is nane for my men and me.

A few hundred yards off the A7, on the left, signed for Carlanrig, is the site of Johnnie's grave, with a memorial tablet (there are still plenty of trees around). On the main road there is the privately run Johnnie Armstrong Gallery. The memory of the wild Armstrongs is kept green by the Armstrong Clan Society, but the glamour has come only with the passage of time. The Border Reivers were bandit tribes, living a hard, brutal existence in which treachery, ambush and the double-cross played more part than honour and patriotism.

At Northhouse the A7 crosses the River Teviot. Its broad valley was the home of two great Border families, the Scotts (at the western end) and the Kerrs (at the eastern end). A little way west of here is Harden, where lived Wat Scott of Harden, an ancestor of the novelist Sir Walter Scott. When the larder stocks ran low, his wife, "muckle-mouth'd Meg", used to present him with a dish on which lay a pair of clean spurs. The message was clear. Pride, rivalry and land disputes led to inevitable blood-feuds not only between these families and their supporters, but also between different branches of the same family.

Follow the A7 for about 6 miles to Hawick. The old market town, now a woollens and farming centre, was burned and attacked too often in the past to preserve much trace of the reivers' heyday. Its jail was often crowded. It was here in 1562 that the Earl of Moray, acting on behalf of Queen Mary, had 28 notorious reivers drowned in the Teviot; on another occasion 36 of the Armstrongs were hanged on a single day.

Memories here go beyond the Reiving days to 1513 and the battle of Flodden at which James IV perished with thousands of his countrymen. Drumlanrig's Tower, just beyond the bridge, on the right, was the strong point of the Warden of the Middle March: it is now a visitor centre.

Drumlanrig's Tower, *High Street, Hawick, Roxburghshire; tel 01450 377615* (open April–Sept, Mon–Sat 10am–12noon and 1pm–5pm, Sun 2pm–6pm).

The statue at the other end of the High Street celebrates one of Hawick's great moments, when in 1514 a band of young lads from here, mounted on carthorses, won a spirited skirmish against the English in the year after Scotland's disastrous defeat at Flodden. Stay on the A7 from Hawick, heading northwards for **Selkirk**. Perched on its hill above the Ettrick Water, this small town has seen many events of Scottish history (see Wallace Trail). Its small museum recalls some of them, as does the statue of the standard-bearer in the High Street, said to have been the only man of Selkirk to have returned from the field of Flodden, not far from here, in 1513.

Selkirk, Halliwell's House Museum, *Main Square, Selkirk; tel 01750 20096* (open April–June, Sept–Oct, Mon–Sat 10am–5pm, Sun 2pm–4pm; July–Aug, daily, 10am–6pm).

Selkirk also has the old courtroom where Sir Walter Scott (see Monks of Melrose Trail), the novelist and poet, used to sit as Sheriff of the county. His extraordinary house, **Abbotsford**, is 4 miles north of here. The Reivers' Trail ends at Selkirk. From here, the A7 takes you past Galashiels, the "capital" of the Borders woollen industry and through impressive sweeping hills back to Edinburgh (about 38 miles).

Recommended Reading: *The Steel Bonnets* by George Macdonald Fraser

TRAIL 14

"In My End Is My Beginning" – The Trail of Mary, Queen of Scots

Two days, from Edinburgh

Mary Stewart, daughter of King James V, born in Linlithgow Palace in 1542 and beheaded at Fotheringay Castle in England in 1587, is the only queen to have ruled Scotland in her own right before the 'Union of the Crowns' in 1603. Her eventful and tragic life has inspired dramas, operas, novels and a host of biographies. Today as in her own time, she still inspires strong emotions. Some see her as a clever woman let down by the incompetence of the men about her; others see a pleasure-loving, foolish woman hopelessly out of her depth in the jungle of Scottish politics. All agree that she was someone of exceptional glamour: tall, handsome, regal, and yet with a strong impulsive streak.

This trail starts geographically at Newhaven harbour, just west of Leith on the Edinburgh shoreline; and historically on a misty morning in August 1561. The 'haar', a chill North Sea mist which sometimes cloaks the city, kept things dim and hazy as the Queen of Scots landed from a French ship. She had been Queen of France until her sickly young husband, King Louis, had died. Now a widow, though only 18, she was seeing her homeland for the first time since she had been sent to France for her own safety as a child of 6. There were loyal cheers but also grim and anxious faces. Scotland was plunging ahead into the revolution created by the religious Reformation. Mary was a Catholic queen, come to rule a turbulent land where militant Protestants were determined not to allow any backsliding. She actually landed at Leith, but the small harbour at Newhaven, built by her grandfather, James IV, and now overlooked by a 19th-century lighthouse, gives a better notion of the port of 1561 than the modern Leith Docks. Newhaven can be reached by following signs to Leith, then driving for a mile parallel to the sea along Commercial Road. It is also a bus-route destination.

The queen was conveyed from the harbour to her new home, Holyrood Palace in Edinburgh. Of the outside of the building you see now, only the north-west towers, with their chateau-like spires and their heraldic signs set in the stone walls, remain from that time. The parkland around the palace was a royal hunting ground, and this would have pleased Mary, who enjoyed country sports and was an accomplished rider. To the west was the long street that led uphill towards the city and the castle. Up there lived the spokesman of the Protestants, the formidable preacher John Knox, once a Catholic priest and now the dedicated foe of Rome. The house in the High Street which bears his name was only briefly occupied by him, but it remains a memento of its time. There were long debates with Knox, which sometimes reduced her to tears. "Never was a sovereign so hardly used," she said. From such pressures, the still-teenaged queen would sometimes slip out in the evening dusk, dressed as a young man, with only one or two of her attendants. For a short time she could savour the pleasures of anonymity as one of the crowd in the narrow streets that at that time clustered around the end of the Canongate.

Inside the palace, terrors lay in wait as well as delights. Beneath the east window of the now-ruined Chapel Royal she married Henry, Lord Darnley in July 1565. It was a Catholic ceremony with fine music and all the ritual that Knox deplored. Less than two years later, Darnley's strangled corpse

The Palace of Holyroodhouse, Edinburgh

was to be buried in the same chapel. In the older part of the palace is the original, reassembled interior of the room where on 9 March 1566, the queen, seven months pregnant, sat screaming as her husband, "King" Henry, with two accomplices, burst in to drag out her confidential secretary David Riccio and stab him to death, throwing his corpse, with fifty-six wounds, down the staircase.

After that, it was within the security of the castle walls that she gave birth to a son, the future James VI, on 19 June. The room, in the castle's south-east range, is preserved. The initials H. and M. over the doorway are those of his father and mother; and his and his mother's coats of arms are in the ceiling. (Despite this filial display, James did nothing for his mother when she was an English prisoner: "Let her drink the ale she brewed" was his comment.)

Edinburgh, Palace of Holyroodhouse, *Canongate, Edinburgh; tel 0131 556 7371* (open April–Oct, daily, 9.30am–6pm; Nov–March, daily, 9.30am–4.30pm).

John Knox's House, *High Street, Edinburgh; tel 0131 556 2647* (open all year, Mon–Sat 10am–4.30pm).

Having come upon Mary already in mid-career, the trail now takes you to the place of her birth. Leave Edinburgh by the M8, signed for Glasgow, and after 2 miles, turn on to the M9, signed for Stirling, and follow this to Junction 3 (7 miles) where you turn off towards Linlithgow (2 miles). This town stretches along a single lengthy street, and in the midde, by a little square on the right-hand side, is Linlithgow Palace. Now a vast and imposing ruin, sited on green slopes above a small loch, this was where Mary was born to her French mother, Mary of Guise, on 8 December 1542.

Linlithgow Palace, *Linlithgow, West Lothian; tel 01506 842896* (open daily, April–Sept, 9.30am–6.30pm; Oct–March, Mon–Sat 9.30am–4.30pm, Sun 2pm–4.30pm).

Very soon after, the infant queen was taken to Stirling Castle, always the safest place for Scottish monarchs. There she was crowned, the too-large crown being held over her head by the Earl of Arran, who was acting as Regent. Stirling was where she grew up, in the new palace completed within the castle walls by her father (see Trail of Royal Scotland). When Henry VIII of England invaded in the ferocious campaign known as the "rough wooing" (he wanted Mary to marry his son), even Stirling was felt to be unsafe. The girl queen was taken once to Dunkeld, to the bishop's house by the cathedral (see Trail of Rob Roy). After the Scottish defeat at Pinkie in 1547, Mary was taken westwards.

Closely following her own route, the trail leaves Stirling on the A84, signed for Crianlarich, and follows it to Doune, turning right in the centre on to the A820, and following it to the edge of town and Doune Castle (on the right). The name of this small town means "fort", and it is likely that on her way west, Mary spent a night in this massively walled castle. Once the stronghold of Murdoch Stewart, Duke of Albany, in the 15th century, it commanded the road westwards. Built above the River Teith just where it is joined by the Ardoch, the walls of its great tower are over 10 feet thick.

Doune Castle, *Doune, Perthshire; tel 01786 841742* (open daily, April–Sept, 9.30am–6pm; Oct–March, Mon–Wed and Sat 9.30am–4.30pm, Thurs and Sun 2pm–4.30pm).

From the castle, return through Doune and turn left on to the A884, then after about half a mile, right on to the B826. Follow this road until it meets the A873, and turn right on to this road, through the village of Thornhill (5 miles), with its zigzag bends, and continue for a further 5 miles, skirting the level expanse of Flanders Moss. In the mid 16th century this area was a mixture of heath and marsh, rough country that was dangerous without a guide. At Port of Menteith, turn left on to the B8034 for about a quarter of a mile, and park at the car park for the ferry.

Here you are overlooking the Lake of Menteith. It was to the wooded island of Inchmahome that the queen was taken. Even now it feels far from anywhere else; at that time it was truly remote, protected by marsh and mountain. The island priory (now ruined) was her home from September 1547 to July 1548. The little garden she tended, called "Queen Mary's Bower", is still to be seen on the island. Follow the instructions for signalling to the ferryboat. Ideally it should have oars, but even the buzz of its outboard motor cannot impair the tranquillity of this place. The island's name means "isle of St Colmac"; the priory, founded in 1238 and once patronised by the Stewarts, was later owned by the Grahams, and the writer R.B. Cunninghame Graham is buried in the ruined nave. On a tiny island west of Inchmahome are the remains of a castle. This loch, known as "the only lake in Scotland", bears the name of "lake" in error; the fact that the surrounding area is known as the "Laigh" (lowland) of Menteith made some people think that the reference was to a lake.

Inchmahome Priory, *Lake of Menteith, Stirlingshire; tel 01877 385294* (open daily, April–Sept, 9.30am–6.30pm; 5-minute ferry included in entry price).

In the summer of 1548, Mary was taken from here to Dumbarton, where a French ship was waiting to take her to France. Return to the A81, and turn left for Aberfoyle (see Trail of Rob Roy). At the junction with the A821 (4 miles), stay on the A81, turning left for Glasgow, until you reach the junction with the A811 (7 miles). Turn right on to the A811 and pass through the pleasant low hill country south of Loch Lomond to Balloch, where you turn right on the A813 for Dumbarton (the name means "fort of the Britons"). At the roundabout outside the town, head straight across the A82 for the town centre and Dumbarton Rock. Here, under the steep fortress-crowned rock that was once the capital of the kingdom of Strathclyde, the ship waited for five anxious days for a fair wind. The Clyde was then very different from its present industrial and post-industrial appearance. At last conditions were right, and the ship sailed, taking Mary away from her kingdom for 14 years.

Dumbarton Castle, *Dumbarton, West Dunbartonshire; tel 01389 732167* (open daily April–Sept, 9.30am–6pm; Oct–March, Mon–Wed and Sat 9.30am–4.30pm, Thurs and Sun 2pm–4.30pm).

The trail now takes a jump in time, to 1568. Mary has been reigning as queen for seven years, and everything has ended in disaster. Her husband, Darnley, was murdered, at the orders of the Earl of Bothwell, who became her lover and her third husband. But, scandalised at the marriage with Bothwell, only three months after Darnley's death, the nobility of Scotland rose against her. Bothwell fled the country and Mary was

Loch Leven Castle, Loch Leven, Fife

forced to abdicate in favour of her baby son, and imprisoned in a castle on Loch Leven. Escaped from there, she rallied her supporters, but their strength was not so great as that of her opponents. At the Battle of Langside, on 14 May 1568, it all came to an end.

To reach the Langside battlefield site, now covered by the suburban sprawl of Glasgow, from Dumbarton, follow Glasgow signs to the A82 and continue on this road as far as Old Kilpatrick (5 miles), then turn left for the Erskine Bridge (A898 then M898), and join the M8 Glasgow-bound at Junction 30. At Junction 24 (10 miles) turn off the motorway, turn right into Helen Street over the motorway bridge, and left on to the A761, signed for City Centre. Take the first right off this elevated road, on to the B768 (Dumbreck Road). You follow the B768 all the way to Langside, crossing the M77 motorway and passing along Titwood Road, with Crossmyloof Station on the right, bearing right down Minard Road, which becomes Langside Avenue, as far as Battle Place. Park in a side street here. Battlefield Road runs from here towards Mount Florida, then known as Clincart Hill, where Mary stood (there is a commemorative stone at the "Court Knowe").

The battle was brief. Battlefield Road, then a country lane between two low hills, separated the Queen's army from that of the Regent. Mary's force advanced down from Clincart Hill and there was intensive hand-to-hand fighting, but the Queen's men were driven back, with the final push given by a Highland charge. Mary's last die had been cast. With a handful of supporters, she rode south, to throw herself on the mercy of her royal cousin Elizabeth.

The Queen Mary trail however goes backwards in time at this point, returning to the east side of Scotland. Retrace your way by the B768 to the M8 and follow the motorway through central Glasgow, as far as Junction 13 (7 miles), where you turn off on to the M80, signed for Stirling, and follow it to Junction 5 (about 18 miles), turning off there for the M876, signed to Kincardine bridge (10 miles). At Kincardine take the A977 from the roundabout, signed for Kinross (11 miles). "Kinross" means "head of the promontory", and as you drive into the town centre and on towards the pier, you will see that it is indeed on a headland which juts into a broad loch. About half a mile from the tip of the headland is a small island clad with trees, among which can be seen the wall of a small castle. It is here that Mary was imprisoned for eleven months after being captured by the regent's forces in 1567: a less pleasant island sojourn than that of Menteith.

At this point among all the extraordinary events of Mary's life, her story most seems to come straight from the pages of a historical romance. She charmed the son of the castle's keeper on to her side, and a daring plan was laid. A young confederate, the 18-year-old Willie Douglas, stole the castle keys, escorted the queen, dressed as a countrywoman, to a boat. He locked the gate and threw the keys into the loch, then rowed her across the loch to where a little group of supporters were waiting. For a brief time, hopes were high. Alas for Mary, the bold escape was to lead in thirteen days' time to the final defeat at Langside.

The castle is a very simple one, a square tower surrounded by a rampart, with its door set high in the wall. The queen herself was confined in a round turret set in the angle of the walls, 15 feet in diameter, with a fireplace and a single window. Here on 23 July 1567, she was forced to sign her abdication.

Loch Leven Castle, *Kinross, Perth & Kinross; tel 01386 040483* (open April–Sept, 9.30am–6.30pm; ferry 5 minutes, price included in admission fee).

From Kinross, drive west to the M90 and join it at Junction 6 (half a mile), in the direction of Edinburgh (24 miles).

Recommended Reading: *Mary Queen of Scots* by Antonia Fraser

TRAIL 15

Coal and Culture: Culross and Bo'ness

One day, from Edinburgh or Glasgow

Deep in the rocks that underlie the Firth of Forth are coal seams, laid down when Scotland was a pre-Jurassic jungle of great forest trees. Where it comes near the surface, this coal has been mined for hundreds of years. Mining was once a major industry, but now only one or two deep pits survive. This trail takes you back in time to the era of the mining pioneers, and then to the heyday of coal and steam in the 19th century.

Leave Edinburgh on the A90 Forth Bridge road, cross the bridge (toll) and turn off left at Junction 1 on to the A985, signed for Kincardine Bridge. At Torryburn (13 miles) turn left on to the B9037 for Culross. You are passing through a landscape marked by industry; even the name of one village by the sea, Limekilns, expresses an industrial purpose. Hidden between the B9037 and the sea is a great expanse of ash fields, residues from the furnaces of coal-burning power stations.

As the road meets the edge of the sea, you enter Culross, whose central area holds perhaps the best-conserved old town in Scotland, rescued in 1932 from a state verging on collapse and demolition. It is a tiny place but rich in associations. Park in the car park at the far end of the village, by the side of an old ice-house, and stroll back. The green foreshore here was once a port for small ships, which sat on the beach at low tide; the little town prospered on coal, salt-panning, hand-loom weaving and the making of "girdles" (flat iron cooking pans for use over the fire) until the larger-scale industry of the late 18th century overtook it and left it to decline.

In the 6th century, it was an important religious site. St Thenew, whose name has been masculinised into St Enoch, was shipwrecked here and here her son, St Mungo, Glasgow's patron saint, was born. The religious community became an abbey in 1217. With its stony streets and the irregularly placed houses, Culross shows what other towns were also like in the late 16th century. The white-walled houses sometimes look almost like sculptural forms. Their outer coat of "harling" covers up the rough free-stone walls and makes them wind- and weather-proof. It also gave the occupants a chance to express a sense of colour, as you will see in the ochre-tinted "palace". This striking building, looking rather like an old French chateau, was the home of a great entrepreneur, Sir George Bruce. His fortune was based on coal and he was one of the first constructors of an under-sea mine, with a pumping system to keep its shafts clear of water. A walk through the palace rooms and a tour of its garden give you a clear insight into the life of a prosperous household at the end of the 16th century.

This building, the old Town House, and the house known as the "study", are all maintained by the National Trust for Scotland and a single ticket serves for all three. Most of the old houses are in private occupancy, but you see all the typical features of Scottish vernacular or "native" architecture; the crow-step gables, the outside staircases, the dormer roof windows (of which Culross Palace's were among the first), the built-out turrets of larger houses like the "study".

Directly across the firth is the harbour of Bo'ness, your next destination. Upstream from it lies the petro-chemical complex of Grangemouth; on your own side the high stack of a power station rises to the right. This region is still one of the main engine-rooms of modern Scotland.

From the cobbled main square, walk or drive up past the mercat (market) cross to the abbey. The restored church rises above the massive ruins of the old monastic buildings. In the chapel of the north side stands the elaborate tomb of Sir George Bruce and his wife, with statues of their eight children kneeling in prayer at the front. Before Bruce's time, the abbey itself owned the right to mine coal here; his ornate monument signals a new order in Scottish life, the rise of a capitalist economy – the father of modern economics, Adam Smith, (1723–90) author of The Wealth of Nations, was born at Kirkcaldy, 20 miles along the coast. Sir George's miners were virtually serfs, forbidden by law to leave or to follow any other trade. Whole families, men, women and children, worked to hack out and bring up the coal in conditions which were only tolerable because they had never experienced anything else. The "palace" had its human price.

Culross, Palace, Study and Town House, *National Trust for Scotland, The Palace, Culross, Fife; tel 01383 880359* (open, April–May and Sept, daily, 1pm–5pm; June–Aug, daily, 10am–5pm; Oct, Sat–Sun 1pm–5pm).

Follow the minor road inland from the abbey to the junction with the A985, where you turn left for Kincardine Bridge (4 miles).

For a little diversion (4 miles each way) take the A977, then the A907 leftwards, to Clackmannan, in the tiny former county of Clackmannanshire. It has always been a quiet place; the 19th-century poet W.E. Aytoun said "nobody has ever been there". The name means "stone of Manan", and refers to an ancient stone dedicated to the Celtic god Manan. The stone itself is at the top of the wide main street, where in 1833 it was set up on a shaft of rock, just by the old tolbooth. To the post-Freudian eye it looks distinctly like a phallic symbol. The tolbooth tower, with its 8th-century "helmet", is of the same design as that of Culross.

The trail takes you across the swing-bridge at Kincardine and on the short M876 motorway, joining the M9 at Junction 7 in the direction of Edinburgh. Leave the motorway at Junction 5, taking the A905, then the A904, into Bo'ness (6 miles). Just past the motorway junction is the site of a Roman camp; the eastern end of the Antonine Wall, built around AD 143 in a vain attempt to keep the northern tribesmen at bay, was here; the place-name Kinneil is from the Gaelic for "wall's end". Bo'ness is a shortened form of Borrowstounness, meaning walled town on the headland. From the seafront here you can see the white houses of Culross, 2 miles away as the seagull flies.

From its medieval origins, Bo'ness grew as a coal mining and exporting town, and a centre of other industries. You can see one of these in action at the Birkhill Fireclay Mine, at Kinneil. Access to this is only via a flight of steps down into the river gorge. The tour takes about an hour and the temperature within the mine is cool, so warm clothing is desirable. Close by is the mansion of Kinneil House, begun in 1553 by the Earl of Arran, then Regent of Scotland, and still with 16th-century wall-paintings in two rooms, though the building was much altered in 1677 (public access to the grounds only). Down by the sea, the old railway station has been preserved as part of the Bo'ness and Kinneil Railway, which runs steam trains out to the Birkhill Mine (combined ticket can be bought) and has a fine collection of old railway artifacts both outside and in an exhibition hall.

Bo'ness Station, *Union Street, Bo'ness, West Lothian; tel 01506 822298* (exhibition open daily July–Aug, 11.30am–5pm).

Birkhill Fireclay Mine, *Birkhill, Bo'ness, West Lothian; tel 01506 822298* (telephone to confirm opening times, or check with tourism information office, 01506 826626, April–Sept).

As you leave Bo'ness by the A994 for Edinburgh, another short diversion (2 miles each way) takes you on to the B903 to Blackness Castle, a wedge-shaped castle perched on a rocky outcrop right at the edge of the sea. Built in the 1440s but very much enlarged and altered in the 16th century, this has been a royal castle since 1453, used more as a fort and jail than as a house. It has a grim lower prison at sea level where the chill waters of the incoming tide rise through a grating to partially flood the cell. There was much parleying and skirmishing round here in 1488, in the revolt against King James III, which cost the king his life and brought his son James IV to the throne.

Blackness Castle, *Blackness, Linlithgow, West Lothian; tel 01506 834807* (open April–Sept, Mon–Sat 9.30am–6.30pm, Sun 2pm–6.30pm; Oct–March, Mon–Wed 9.30am–4.30pm, Sun 2pm–4.30pm).

To return to Edinburgh, go back to the A994, turning left; follow it to Junction 3 of the M9, and join the motorway following the signs to Edinburgh (15 miles).

The Town House, Culross, Fife

TRAIL 16

The Beginnings of Geology: Hugh Miller's Cromarty, and Knockan Cliff, where the Uniformitarians knocked out the Catastrophists

One and a half days, from Inverness

DAY ONE

It was in Scotland, in the last years of the 18th century and the first half of the 19th, that the modern science of Geology began. Edinburgh had developed a strong scientific tradition, and one of the leading men was James Hutton (1726–1797). Trained as a physician, he became more interested in chemistry, and after inheriting a small farm in the Borders, he became interested in the chemistry of the soil and then in the origin of land-forms. In 1785, Hutton delivered a paper, "The Theory of the Earth", to the Royal Society of Edinburgh. For the first time, the principles of erosion and stratification were laid down. Hutton also believed that the core of the earth was a fiery liquid. He and his supporters were dubbed "the Plutonians".

The work of the geologists had consequences that they did not foresee. It became clear that the earth was far older than had been supposed (the most widely accepted estimate up till then was that the world had been created in 4004 BC – a million times out). More seriously, the traditional Biblical account of creation was threatened by the revelation of the fossil record, and what it implied in terms of time. By 1834, when the Geological Society of Edinburgh was founded, numerous Scots had already established geology as an important science that revolutionised the way people thought of the world. It was not done without pain, as the first part of our Geology Trail reveals.

Leave Inverness on the northbound A9, signposted for Wick, and cross the Beauly Firth on a high bridge to reach the fertile, wooded peninsula known as the "Black Isle". At the roundabout of Tore (7 miles), turn right on to the A832, signed for Cromarty ("Crooked Bay"). Follow this road for 18 miles to Cromarty, a well-preserved old seaport town, once a county capital. The vast anchorage enclosed behind its twin headlands was once a naval base, a home of the Grand Fleet, but nowadays is a haven for oil rigs and their support vessels. With its knot of old streets and its handsome 18th-century buildings, the quiet little town is an agreeable place; fishing nets for catching salmon still hang up to dry on its eastern foreshore.

Among the Georgian town houses, with their handsome, sober facades and slate roofs, is a humbler whitewashed and thatched cottage, preserved as the birthplace and boyhood home of Hugh Miller (1802–1856). Orphaned at five, he was brought up by his uncles and apprenticed as a stonemason. But his interest in stones went far beyond chiselling them. As a child he had scrambled about on the beach and been intrigued by fossils. Later he walked to the Eathie Burn, up in the hill behind the town, and found more fish fossils in the little gorge it had cut in the Old Red Sandstone rocks. His geological researches resulted in a book, *The Old Red Sandstone* (1841), a pioneering work of geology that inspired several later generations of field-workers. Miller was also strongly religious. In later life he moved to Edinburgh, where he became editor of the influential *Witness* newspaper, combining social and religious commentary with his continuing geological research. But the intellectual and spiritual struggle between his religious beliefs and his scientific discoveries proved to be unbridgeable, and he shot himself on Christmas Eve 1856.

Miller's little house with its mementoes is a poignant reminder of the stresses that the great discoveries of the 19th century brought with them; it is also a reminder of a one-time "traditional" Scottish type, the poor village boy who, fired by natural genius, triumphs over difficulties to make a distinguished career. If you have done, or do, the Wallace Trail, you will see his craggy bust in the "hall of heroes" in the National Wallace Monument at Stirling.

Hugh Miller's House, *Cromarty, Ross-shire; tel 01381 600245* (open April–Sept, Mon–Sat 10am–12noon and 1pm–5pm, Sun 2pm–5pm).

On the return route to Inverness, as the A832 climbs up from Cromarty, you will pass a very minor road signposted to Eathie on the left. At Upper Eathie it passes the head of the valley where young Miller went fossil-hunting. Equipped with stout shoes, you can follow the moist, thickly wooded ravine for some way, but beware of steep slopes as it drops towards the sea. From the little road there are also fine views southwards across the narrow part of Moray Firth, towards the Cairngorm Mountains.

DAY TWO

Leave Inverness again by the northbound A9, but this time turn off left at Tore (7 miles), on to the A835, signed to Ullapool (52 miles). As this is a "geological" trail, look out for the transition from the gently rounded, fertile green farmland of the Old Red Sandstone on the eastern coast, to the rugged, rocky, heath-covered landscape of the interior, the surface of ancient hard rocks producing a thin, acidic soil. The village of Contin (7 miles from Tore) is the gateway: you enter by green fields and leave among rocks and thickets. Two miles on, the Falls of Rogie come tumbling off the hard rocks known as Moine schists (Moine is Gaelic for "moor"). There is a car park and the falls are only two or three minutes' walk.

This clearly is glaciated country, with its wide U-shaped valleys, glacier-cut, between mountains which have been rounded down by the vast weight and slow movement of the ice sheet. There is much evidence of hummocky deposits of soil and great boulders left by the retreating glaciers (the last glaciation ended as recently – in geological time – as 12,000 years ago). Winding through this rough landscape, you reach Garve (from Gaelic garbh, "rough") and follow the A835, to the right, at the junction west of the village, beneath the high ridge of Ben Wyvis. The road passes a dam built for hydro-electric purposes, with a complex of mountains rising from the western end of the artifical loch. The wild landscape of peat bog and water traversed by the road is known as the Dirie Mhor (pronounced Jeerie Vore, Gaelic for "great climb").

Dropping from the watershed, with the streams now flowing west, you come past Braemore road junction to the great chasm of Corriehalloch, where the River Droma drops 200 feet at the Falls of Measach into a narrow gorge, probably originally formed by the much larger torrent pouring off the gradually melting ice-sheet. The car park is on the right-hand side of the road; to the left a well-made short path leads down through the trees to a viewing platform and a spectacular foot-bridge. Two miles on, you see the glint of water. Although the open sea is 20 miles away, this is the tip of Loch Broom, an arm of the sea reaching far inland. Presently Ullapool comes in sight, distinctively placed on a raised beach which shows how far the land has "bounced" back from the sea level of the Ice Age (north-west Scotland is still rising, at a microscopic pace, out of the sea). Deepened by glaciers cutting into its rock floor, Loch Broom's fiord-like form is typical of many western sea-lochs.

Ullapool (the name, "Olaf's farmstead", is from the Norse occupancy of northern Scotland, from around AD 900–1100) is the ferry-port for Lewis, a fishing harbour and tourist centre, with a pleasantly informal local museum. Still on the Geology Trail, the A835 swings north into a landscape quite different to the gloomy moors of the Dirie Mhor. At Ardmair, a crescent beach of pebbles sometimes yields semi-precious stones, whilst above it rises the dramatic cliff-face of Ben More Coigach. Your road seeks the ways of least resistance, wriggling between the Cromalt Hills to the right and the strange-shaped, steep mountains of Coigach on the left. Past the junction of the narrow road leading to Achiltibuie and the Summer Isles, you come to Knockan ("little hill") about 13 miles from Ullapool, a place of pilgrimage for the world's geologists.

Here it was shown definitively, for the first time, in 1883, that older rocks can be found on top of more recent rocks, as a result of movements and upheavals of the earth's crust. An end was put to the dispute between the "Catastrophists", who believed that the earth's surface had changed little since its formation in a series of vast explosive events, and the "Uniformitarians", now shown to be correct, who believed that the landscape was in constant process of re-formation.

The gradual seismic shift that took place here, some 400 million years ago, was called the Moine Thrust. To the west are the extremely ancient (2.7 billion years) rocks of Lewisian gneiss, the oldest rocks in Europe, topped with Torridonian sandstone (around 700 million years old), much of it scraped right off, but with remnants still forming distinctive mountain shapes; to the east is the kind of Moinian schist (around 600 million years old) forming the landscape you drove through on the way across country. The thrust itself happened as the mountains to the east were being formed. The pressure against the immensely resistant gneiss "foreland" resulted in the Moine schists being forced up and over much younger rocks, or displacing areas of older rocks, so that the layers of rock in some places have been "re-shuffled".

The process has been fully worked out here, and a walk around the Knockan Cliff Nature Trail (one hour plus some steep paths, but with ladders and footboards at steepest and wettest points) enables you to see the effects at close-up, including how the movement of two massive planes of rock grinds their meeting edges into a sort of natural mortar. In clear weather there are superb views of the neighbouring mountains from the cliff top. The little visitor centre here (summer only) has useful information. Other rock types in this region include the quartzite rocks that can be seen capping such ancient sandstone mountains as Canisp and Quinag, and the limestone that comes to the surface 12 miles further north at Inchnadamph, both dating from the Cambrian era, 570 million years ago.

You are in a region full of interest not only in terms of geology but also of natural history; but on a one-day trail, it is time to return to Inverness, by a choice of routes. Return by the way you came, or go 3 miles north on the A835 to Ledmore, and turn right on to the narrow A837 which crosses the rugged county of Sutherland, following the River Oykell eastwards, and joins the A836 at Inveran. Here you are very close to some of the sites on the Sutherland Clearance Trail. At Bonar Bridge the narrow Kyle of Sutherland is crossed and you follow the south side of the Dornoch Firth, a river valley deepened by ice and invaded by the sea, to join the A9 close to the historic little town of Tain, once a place of pilgrimage for King James IV. Here you are back in the sandstone farmlands of the eastern coast, and the road sweeps through the green countryside, with the hills on the right reaching almost to the sea in places, before swinging southwards to cross the Cromarty Firth on a long, low bridge and the Beauly Firth on the high bridge which you have already crossed in the other direction, to reach Inverness (92 miles).

TRAIL 17

The Trail of Robert Burns

Two Days in the Burns Country

The "cult" of Robert Burns (1759–1796) began very soon after his death. Illness, caused by childhood hard work and made worse by lack of medical knowledge, killed him while still at the height of his powers as a poet. Very soon the Scots realised that they had lost someone very remarkable. The cottage built by his father, where he was born, was preserved, and all over south-west Scotland memorials large and small indicate his presence and his fame. You may agree, as you experience the Burns "industry", with the remark of the English poet, John Keats, an early visitor, that there is a lot of "cant and flummery" about a birthplace. But as you explore this green countryside, with its old-fashioned country towns and villages, you will get nearer to the man himself, who loved this region with its clear sparkling rivers and its green slopes.

The trail sets off from Glasgow, and its early part can be combined with that of the Wallace Trail (see page 20). Alternatively, leave the city on the M77, signposted for **Kilmarnock** (30 miles).

This town has grown greatly since Burns's day and its old centre has been almost entirely obliterated by 19th- and 20th-century developments. Parking in the centre is confined to specified car parks (timed ticket meters). Burns had strong connections with Kilmarnock, the chief one being that it was here the first edition of his poems was printed and published by John Wilson. In the town centre, Kilmarnock Cross, is a modern statue of Burns and Wilson, erected in 1995. Just west of here at the Laigh ("Low") Church, Burns's friend Tam Samson is buried in the graveyard, with Burns's "Epitaph", composed while the subject was still alive, carved on the stone. North-east of the centre (follow the B7082 along Strawberrybank Road) is Kay's Park, where a turreted and pin-nacled monument (1879) about 70 feet high houses a statue of the poet and a mini-museum. Access to this can be gained by telephoning (in advance) 01563 570624.

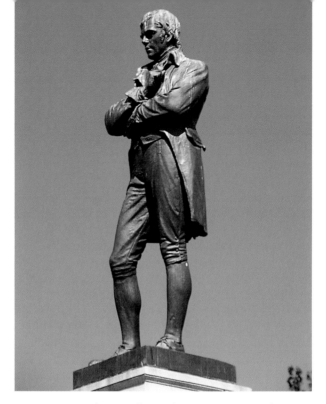

*Robert Burns
Statue, Ayr,
Ayrshire*

Leave Kilmarnock on the A71 signposted to Irvine (10 miles). When Burns was 22, he came here to learn the art of flax-dressing. He detested this and spent his time in a bookshop, courting girls, and writing poems, returning to the family farm of Lochlea in the following year.

Follow the A71 over the interchange with the A78, and turn off to the right at the first roundabout, then to the left at the next roundabout. This takes you into the street known as Townhead. There are several parking areas here, just by the centre of the town. On the north side of the street, just where Townhead becomes High Street, is the narrow Glasgow Vennel, where Burns both lodged and worked. The flax-heckling workshop which the poet so sincerely loathed has been restored, as has the house (No 4) where he is said to have lodged. It has "R.B. 1782" carved above a door, but this is almost certainly not done by Burns himself. Continue along the High Street to Eglinton Street, where the Irvine Burns Club (the oldest Burns Club in the world) maintains a museum at No 28, "Wellwood", a house dedicated to the poet's memory. Although Irvine itself is now a modern industrial town, parts of the central area have been attractively restored to give a sense of the burgh's history. Irvine also has one of the better-done Burns statues, by James Pittendrigh MacGillivray in 1896, overlooking the east bank of the river, by the railway station.

Vennel Museum and Heckling Shop, *4 and 10 Glasgow Vennel, Irvine, Ayrshire; tel 01294 275059* (open all year, Mon–Sat 10am–4pm).

Irvine Burns Club, *"Wellwood", 28 Eglinton St, Irvine;* www.irvineburns.ndirect.co.uk (contact to check opening times).

A non-Burnsian side-attraction here is the Scottish Maritime Museum, at the harbour.

From Irvine the trail goes south by the A78, past the championship golf course at Troon, and joining the A77 north of Ayr. This town played an important part in young Robert's life. He was born just 2 miles away and Ayr was the market town. A small town in Burns's day, it grew greatly in the 19th century, and many of the buildings known to the poet were knocked down. One that remains is the Tam o' Shanter Inn on High Street, which claims to be the tavern from which the drunken Tam, in one of Burns's most celebrated poems, set off on the ride home in which he met the witch "Cutty Sark". The Auld Kirk ("old church") between the High Street and the river, was attended by Burns with his parents when he was a boy, and its graveyard offers a guide to Burns-related graves. Burns liked Ayr:

Auld Ayr, wham ne'er a toon surpasses
For honest men and bonny lasses

He wrote an entertaining poem, "The Twa Brigs", in the form of a dialogue between the old 13th-century bridge and the – to him – new bridge of the town, which prophesied that the old one would outlast the new one, which it did. The new bridge was destroyed by a flood in 1877 and the present one is its replacement. Ayr has its Burns statue in Burns Statue Square, at the foot of Alloway Street, the south-western extension of the High Street, by the railway station.

The B7024 to Alloway leads southwards from Ayr, signposted for Maybole, but you will also see signs for "The

Tam o' Shanter Experience" and Burns National Heritage Park. There are two free car parks, one close to the Burns Cottage, the other adjacent to the "Experience". A signposted footpath leads you between the different elements in the "National Heritage Park" which include the Burns Memorial, the ruined Auld Kirk of Alloway, the Brig o' Doon and the attractive gardens on the riverside.

These elements, set among suburban villas, trees and tennis courts, result from the fact that here is both the place where Burns was born, and the landscape of his comic epic "Tam o' Shanter", whose hero rides from a tavern in Ayr past "Alloway's auld haunted kirk", where he looks in on a witches' revel where the devil is playing the bagpipes. Tam's loud appreciation of the comely young witch Nannie in her short shift or "cutty sark" is noticed; they chase after him in a wild race. In the nick of time he reaches the bridge over the River Doon, since "A runnin' stream they daurna cross", and Nannie, cheated of her victim, is left clutching only the tail of Tam's grey mare. The Centre provides an audio-visual presentation on the poem and on Burns, though it must be said that the apparent emphasis is more upon the shop, with a vast range of Burns-related merchandise.

Close by is the steep-banked Doon valley, hymned by Burns in the haunting song *Ye Banks and Braes o' Bonnie Doon*, above which rises the best-known and perhaps the most attractive of the Burns monuments, a classically styled pillared circular canopy set on a three-sided base. The surrounding gardens contain engaging statues of Burns characters by a local sculptor, James Thom (1799–1850), who later made good in the USA.

The museum adjoining the Burns Cottage has a very good collection of Burns material. The Cottage itself has been restored, though it hardly needs the placard on the roof: its long, low shape is distinctive among the more recent stone houses. Quite apart from its Burns associations, including the memorable night when he was only a few days old and the wind blew down part of the roof and the southern gable, it represents a style of building that was once universal in southern Scotland and is now hardly to be seen anywhere else.

Alloway, Burns National Heritage Park, *Murdoch's Lane, Alloway, Ayr; tel 01292 443700.*

Burns Cottage and Museum, open April–Oct daily, 9am–6pm; Nov–March, Mon–Sat 10am–4pm, Sun 12 noon–4pm
Burns Monument and Gardens (open June–Aug daily, 9am–7pm; April–May and Sept–Oct, Mon–Sat 10am–5pm, Sun 2pm–5pm; Nov–March, Mon–Sat 10am–4pm).
Tam o' Shanter Experience (open April–Oct, 9am–6pm; Nov–March, Mon–Sat 9am–5pm).

The Old Brig o' Doon and the Auld Kirk at Alloway are open at all times without charge. The Auld Kirk shows the grave of William Burnes, the poet's father, and other members of the family.

The Burns family left Alloway when Robert was 7 years old, on the first of a series of failed efforts made by his father, then by himself, to earn a living by farming. Drive from Alloway on the minor road towards the A77 and cross it towards Corton; the road to Mount Oliphant (two and a half miles) branches off to the right. The farms lived in by Burns are now much enlarged and improved places, but it was during the family's ten years on this exposed hillside that the growing boy, struggling with the horse-drawn plough, laid also the seeds of the rheumatic fever and endocarditis that would cause his premature death. From Mount Oliphant, return to the Corton road, turn right over the railway line and on to join the A713 (about one and a half miles); after a short distance turn left on to the B742, and follow this through the undulating countryside past Annbank to turn right on to the B744 for Tarbolton. Turn left into the village, and right at the bottom of the main street, by the church, into Sandgate, to park in a few yards by the white-walled "Bachelors' Club" on the right-hand side.

In 1777 Burns's father moved again, to Lochlea Farm, two and a half miles from here, and this weavers' village and the nearby little town of Mauchline were the scene of Burns's boisterous late adolescence and early manhood. At the age of 19 he defied his stern father to attend dancing classes in Tarbolton. In 1780 he and his brother founded the Bachelors' Club here, with a few other young men. They met in an upstairs room of a house, then used as an alehouse, to hold self-improving discussions.

Burns Cottage and Museum, Alloway, Ayrshire

Tarbolton, The Bachelors' Club, *Sandgate, Tarbolton, Ayrshire; tel 01292 541940* (open Easter, May–Sept, daily 1pm–6.30pm; Oct, Sat–Sun 1.30pm–6.30pm).

Lochlea Farm is a mile to the left of the B744 Tarbolton–Galston road, about 2 miles from Tarbolton. Here the Burns family lived from 1777 to 1784, when William Burnes died. There is no longer a loch, but a stream flows from the drained-out hollow; through this little valley, the funeral of Burns's father went on its way back to Alloway, the body carried on a litter between two horses, the people following on foot.

The names of the district, including Mossbog and Boghead, indicate what a poor-soiled and waterlogged place it was in the late 18th century. On their father's death, Robert and his brother became tenants of Mossgiel for four years. Return to the B744, turn left towards Mauchline; Mossgiel Farm (with roadside plaque) on its high, windy ridge is 2 miles further on. The present farmhouse incorporates the much smaller house of Burns's time. Another mile takes you into Mauchline, via the A76.

Just where the roads intersect, is the National Burns Memorial. The tower was opened in May 1898, and the cottages by it are old people's homes subsidised by Burns charities. A sturdy, square, turreted building with balconies on the central storey, its top provides fine views. Unfortunately this "national" monument is not kept open. Access to the little museum inside, and the view of the Burns country, must be sought by a prior call to the South Ayrshire District Council.

Mauchline, National Burns Memorial (for access arrangements, contact South Ayrshire Museums Dept, 01563 570624).

At Tarbolton, you will see that the rules of the Bachelors' Club require a member to be a "professed lover of one or more of the female sex". By the time he was living at Mossgiel, Burns amply fulfilled this requirement. One of his early poems was "The Poet's Greeting to His Bastart Wean" ("bastard child").

Continue down the hill into Mauchline, and park by the central crossroads of this normally quiet little town. On the west side, around the parish church, is a rich collection of Burnsian links. It was here he first met Jean Armour, who was to become his wife. In 1788 he and she set up house together in the house that is now a museum, in Castle Street. Four of Burns's children who died within his lifetime are buried here, as well as numerous people mentioned in his poems and letters (notable graves are specially marked). The churchyard (always open) was also the site of his poem "The Holy Fair". The church itself was built after his time, in 1827, replacing the one in which he and Jean had to stand and do penance for fornication (she bore him five children before their marriage and four after it). Across Loudoun Street is Poosie Nancie's Inn, the location of Burns's splendid cantata or song-cycle, "The Jolly Beggars". It still has the feel of an 18th-century tavern, though modernised, and has a small exhibit of historical items. The castle here, a stone keep dating from the 12th century, was ruinous even in Burns's time, but the house adjoining it was lived in by his patron and friend, Gavin Hamilton, a well-off lawyer. Mary Campbell, the tragic "Highland Mary" whose death while pregnant with his child brought him great remorse, was a nursery-maid here.

Mauchline, Burns House Museum, *Castle St, Mauchline, Ayrshire; tel 01292 288688* (open April–Oct, Mon–Sat 11am–12.30pm and 1.30pm–5.30pm, Sun 2pm–5pm).

In June 1788 Burns left Ayrshire to try his luck on a farm at Ellisland, near Dumfries, more than 40 miles to the south. The conclusion of the Burns Trail is to be found with the Border Reivers Trail (see page 95). From Mauchline, Dumfries is 50 miles south, on the A76 all the way. If you are returning to Glasgow, take the A76 north to join the A77 outside Kilmarnock (10 miles), then the A77 and the M77 into Glasgow (28 miles).

TRAIL 18

Campbell's Kingdom: The Argyll Trail

Three days, from Glasgow

This trail takes you into Argyll ("coastland of the Gael"), home of many clans but dominated ever since the 16th century by the Clan Campbell and its chiefs, successively earls and dukes of Argyll. It also takes you to an earlier time, and the first footholds of the people who gave their name to Scotland.

DAY ONE

The starting point is Glasgow. The best way to leave the city is by the M8 motorway, signposted for Paisley and Greenock, and follow it to Junction 30, where you branch off on the M898 for the Erskine Bridge (toll). This bridge soars above the widening Clyde; immediately afterwards, you turn off left on the A82, signed for **Dumbarton** and Crianlarich. Soon on the left you will see Dumbarton Rock rising by the side of the Clyde. This fortress was the stronghold of the ancient Britons and their kingdom of Strathclyde, where the language was not Gaelic but a form of Old Welsh.

Follow the A82 into the level Vale of Leven and on to the south end of Loch Lomond, with its wide expanse and many wooded islands. Ahead on the far side rises the fine peak of Ben Lomond (2,795ft/974m). Gradually the character of the loch changes to a long, narrow, mountain-hemmed trough. At Tarbet, turn left on the A83. Where you find a place called Tarbet or Tarbert, you will always find that it is on a neck of land between two lochs or seas; it means "portage place" where boats could be dragged overland. Here the portage was from Loch Lomond to the sea at Arrochar on Loch Long. The road skirts the head of Loch Long, sets about climbing up Glen Croe, below the massive ramparts of Ben Arthur and Ben Ime, to the summit aptly called Rest and Be Thankful, then runs down Glen Kinglas to the shore of Loch Fyne. It follows the coastline (you are on the coast though 40 miles from the open sea) round the head of the loch and the little Loch Shira (followers of the Rob Roy Trail may note that the Duke of Argyll gave Rob Roy a "safe house" high up in Glen Shira), and along to a tall, humpback bridge controlled by traffic lights. Going over, in the woods to the right you get a glimpse of turrets. Beyond the bridge a handsome little town is revealed in the distance. You have arrived at Inveraray, in the heart of "Campbell's Kingdom".

In the early Middle Ages, the great clans hereabouts were the MacDougalls and MacDonalds. The MacDonalds, self-styled "Lords of the Isles", ruled what was almost a separate kingdom. The MacDougalls opposed Robert Bruce in 1306, and fell from grace when he achieved power. The MacDonalds ruled their Gaelic empire, stretching from the north of Ireland to here, until 1493. But their power and pretensions could not co-exist with those of the king, and eventually the king prevailed.

The royal cause was consistently helped by a small local clan, the Campbells. They fought for Bruce at Bannockburn in 1314. In 1457 their chief, Colin Campbell, was made Earl of Argyll; in 1483, he was Chancellor of Scotland. Since then, the Campbell chief has always styled himself "MacCailein Mor" – son of Great Colin. In 1500, the second earl was made the king's Lieutenant-General for Argyll and the Isles. The influence, wealth, possessions and numbers of the Campbells grew steadily. Many small clans threw in their lot with them and took on the name, to be under the protection of MacCailein Mor. Using every device of law, along with arranged marriages, threats and open warfare, the Campbells extended their power across a vast extent of mainland and islands, by means of a complex social structure of sub-chiefs and sub-letting tenants, known as "tacksmen".

By the end of the 17th century, the 10th Earl became the first Duke of Argyll. The court had moved to London, but the Campbells – usually – remained in royal favour. It added greatly to Argyll's glamour in London that at home he could call up an army of five thousand warlike Highlanders; from the king's point of view, it was better to have Argyll as his policeman rather than his enemy. Throughout the Jacobite period, the Campbells remained firmly on the side of the Hanoverian kings.

It was the wealth and rents of Argyll and the work of its people that paid for the duke's costly attendance at court, and for the building and rebuilding of Inveraray and the other Campbell castles. Loch Fyne, glittering before the town, was a rich source of herring and other fish, and the earl took his share of every catch. The woods, the mineral resources, the cattle and deer – every product of the vast territory paid its dues to the chief.

The vista of Inveraray you see today is the product of the 18th century, when the old stone "clachan" or village by the castle was knocked down (1743) and the handsome new planned town built to replace it, at a convenient distance. As in a number of Scottish towns, the old jail has been turned into a museum. The rather incongruous tall grey Gothic bell tower houses a fine peal of bells, each dedicated to a Celtic saint. It was begun by the 10th Duke in 1914 as a war memorial, particularly to members of Clan Campbell. The castle, still the home of the Duke of Argyll, is not among the most impressive but has a true "baronial" feel as the centre of a ducal empire, including an armoury with every imaginable kind of battleaxe. **Inveraray Castle**, *Inveraray, Argyll; tel 01499 302203* (open April–June, Mon–Thurs and Sat 10am–1pm and 2pm–5.45pm, Sun 1pm–5.45pm; July–Aug, Mon–Sat 10am–5.45pm, Sun 1pm–5.45pm).

Just off the A83, 6 miles south on the left, is the restored crofting township of Auchindrain, an open-air museum presenting the opposite end of the social scale to the ducal grandeur of Inveraray Castle. Its bright and white interiors, however, belie the smoky atmosphere of the dwellings as they originally were,

Inverary Castle, Inverary, Argyll

when the occupants kept the peat fires going virtually all year round.

Port Ellen, Isle of Islay, Argyll

Auchindrain Township, *Auchindrain, near Inveraray, Argyll; tel 01499 500235* (open April–Sept, daily, 10am–5pm).

Two miles on is Furnace, whose name reveals its history as a place where local charcoal was used to smelt iron in the 18th century. There is more former industry at Crarae, where huge granite quarries were worked. Lochgilphead (24 miles), at the head of a shallow inlet off Loch Fyne, is the local administrative and shopping centre for the area.

Fourteen miles south is Tarbert, a fishing port at the east end of the isthmus that joins Knapdale to Kintyre. The remains of a royal castle rise above the harbour; you can reach it by a few minutes' walk along the signed footpath. Here the road crosses to the west side of the peninsula and 5 miles south is Kennacraig Pier, where the car ferry leaves for Islay.

If time is short, you can omit the day on Islay, and continue the trail northwards again from Kennacraig (see below, Day Three).

DAY TWO

Two ferry routes serve the Isle of Islay from here – a two-hour run to Port Askaig, and a three-hour run to Port Ellen. Both pass through the beautiful West Loch Tarbert and by the tip of the Isle of Gigha before separating to cross the wide Sound of Jura, with fine views over to the Paps of Jura and the lower hills of Islay. Timetable details can be got by calling the ferry terminal (01880 730254, or the website www.calmac.co.uk). If possible take one route out and the other way back; the Islay Trail starts at Port Ellen and goes north to Port Askaig, but of course it can be done in reverse.

This big island, shaped rather like an arrowhead, is important in the history of the Western seaboard. The most prized of the Hebrides for its fertility and mineral wealth, it was here that the Lords of the Isles had their stronghold. Islay is also the source of some of the most impressive and unmistakable malt whiskies, with their "peaty" flavour. It is home to about 3,500 people, spread over its handful of villages. Surprisingly, at Port Ellen you are south of the English border on the eastern coast at Berwick. From this "model village", laid out in 1820, take the road past Laphroaig Distillery (tours by appointment: tel 01496 302400) towards Lagavulin (two and a half miles). Here, apart from the distillery with its tour (by appointment, same telephone number as Laphroaig), are the ruins of Dunnyvaig Castle, a strongly fortified tower of the MacDonalds. It was indeed their last stronghold, destroyed in 1615 in a virtual war between the MacDonald Earl of Antrim and Sir John Campbell of Cawdor.

The next in Port Ellen's clutch of distilleries is Ardbeg. As in other distilleries admission is charged but the cost includes a voucher against a purchase. Six miles further on there is one of Scotland's national treasures in the Kildalton churchyard – a superbly carved Celtic cross of the 9th century (open site).

Ardbeg Distillery, *Port Ellen, Isle of Islay, Argyll; tel 01496 302244* (open all year, Mon–Fri 10am–7pm; June–Sept, open also Sat–Sun 10am–7pm).

Returning to Port Ellen, take the A846 to Bowmore (10 miles), the "capital" with its circular church dominating the wide main street, and another visitable distillery (Bowmore Distillery, tel 01496 810441). About 8 miles away on the A847, round the head of Loch Indaal, is Port Charlotte, which has an attractive Museum of Islay Life, including a collection of stone-carvings.

Museum of Islay Life, *Port Charlotte, Isle of Islay, Argyll; tel 01496 850310* (open Easter–Oct, Mon–Sat 10am–5pm, Sun 2pm–5pm).

From here turn back towards the A846 in the direction of Port Askaig. About 7 miles past the road junction of Bridgend, you come to Loch Finlaggan on the left-hand side. Here is the long-abandoned headquarters of the Lords of the Isles, gradually yielding its secrets to modern archaeology. There is a useful interpretive centre here. A stone-and-timber causeway led on to Eilean Mòr ("big island") with the castle, and on to Eilean na Comhairle ("council island"). There was a semi-regal court here, with its law-officers, priests, bards, historians, doctors, from where messengers and ambassadors went as far as Burgundy, London and Dublin. For 150 years it was a centre of Gaelic culture, with its own music, song and poetry. The atmosphere of Finlaggan is redolent now only of vanished glory, as the wind blows across the empty moors and ripples the surface of the loch.

Even when deprived of their self-appointed Lordship, the MacDonalds remained powerful. But a long feud with the MacLeans from the Isle of Mull devastated most of Islay and reduced the MacDonald fortunes. The Campbells, represented by the Cawdor branch of the family, moved into the power vacuum and by 1615 Islay was part of the Campbell empire. Islay House at the head of Loch Indaal replaced the medieval Finlaggan, which was left to crumble away. In 1726 the island was sold to another Campbell, the wealthy merchant-politician Daniel Campbell of Shawfield, who set about making "improvements"; the island's textile mill is a relic of this. Textiles, whisky and tourism sustain Islay today.

The Finlaggan Trust, *The Cottage, Ballygrant, Isle of Islay, Argyll; tel 01496 810629* (open April–Oct; for times contact Tourism Information Centre at Bowmore, tel 01496 810254).

The road runs down to Port Askaig on the narrow and sometimes turbulent Sound of Islay, facing the Jura mountains; the village has the Bunnahabhainn ("stream-foot") and Caol Ila ("strait of Islay") Distilleries, both visitable. Port Askaig is the ferry-port for the return trip to the mainland.

DAY THREE

Again at Kennacraig Pier, you return up the A83. At Ardrishaig you can see the eastern end of the Crinan Canal, a working museum-piece in itself, beautifully maintained. Built between 1793 and 1801, it was never a commercial success but is still used by fishing and pleasure craft. Its tow-path makes an attractive and easy walk. At Lochgilphead, turn left on to the A816, signed for Crinan and Oban. Two miles out, turn left again at Cairnbaan following the signs to Crinan, crossing the canal. It is worth the short twisty detour to see the toytown harbour of Crinan, with its collection of fishing boats and one or two old steam "puffers". There is also a fine view out to sea, where at the north end of Jura lurks the dangerous Corryvrechan whirlpool, and across to the castle of Duntrune, one of the many (mostly ruined) castles guarding the sea-routes.

Returning from Crinan, turn left on the B8025 at Bellanoch, over the canal and into a suddenly flat terrain, skirting the vast level marsh of the Moine Mhor ("great bog"). Turn right along the first road you come to, and after a mile or so, you will see a low rocky hill rising from the plain, with access from a track that leads off on your right. Follow this to the car park.

Here you are at Dunadd, a place of great symbolic and historic significance. In 503 BC the Scots of Dal Riata in Northern Ireland established a kingdom here, and called it Dalriada after their old home. The fort here was the crowning-place of their kings. On its summit (a stony but not difficult walk, a few minutes from the car park) there can still be seen carvings that formed part of the ritual: a foot-shaped indentation into which the king set his foot, a cup hollowed out of the rock, and a sculptured boar. There are also inscriptions in the ancient Irish Ogam script (very faint). From here the Scots spread eastwards and north. Their language, an early form of Gaelic, spread with them, aided by the fact that they were Christians and it thus became the language of the Gospel for the Picts when they were converted. Eventually the Scots and their language became politically dominant. To outsiders it appeared to be the land of the Scots, and thus it acquired the name of Scotland. As you set your foot in the rock of Dunadd, where the Stone of Destiny may have been brought from Ireland, it is easy to sense this quiet place as a focal point in the development of Scottish history.

Turn right from the access track, and follow the road

to the A816, and turn left. You are still in a region of great historical importance. Three miles on, Kilmartin lies at the centre of some 150 identified prehistoric sites, ranging in age from 5,000 years to the time of the coming of the Scots. The churchyard has a remarkable collection of carved grave-slabs and crosses from medieval times, with some fine crosses in the church (open daily, Easter–Sept, 9.30am–6pm). At Kilmartin House an audio-visual display explains the development of this fascinating area, both in terms of archaeology and landscape.
Kilmartin House Museum of Ancient Culture, *Kilmartin, Argyll; tel 01546 510278; www.kht.org.uk* (open all year, daily, 10am–5.30pm).

Follow the A86 north for 28 miles, sometimes skirting the sea, with views out to the inner islands, sometimes inland among the knolls and low hills. To the western (left-hand) side, the bulk of Ben More on the Isle of Mull appears in view.

If your time allows, branch off after about 18 miles to Kilninver, and follow the B844 down to the "bridge over the Atlantic" crossing the very narrow tidal sound between the mainland and the Island of Seil (4 miles). Old slate diggings have left this island pocketed with holes and pools, but the effect is picturesque and from the film-location village of Easdale (5 miles), on its western rim, there is a fine prospect out to the Firth of Lorne. A brief ferry ride (available more or less "on demand" throughout the day, with some one-hour gaps) takes you from here to Easdale Island with its Folk Museum, established in one of the old quarriers' cottages. This side-excursion will show you how modern island communities maintain themselves.
Easdale Island Folk Museum, *Easdale Island, Argyll; www.easdale.com* (open April–Oct, daily, 10.30am–5.30pm).

Return to the A816 which swoops and winds for the last 10 miles into Oban, the largest town on the west coast north of Glasgow, a busy port and tourist centre, and terminus of a railway line to Glasgow. After the atmospheric spaces you have been visiting, you may find its souvenir shops tawdry and its pavements crowded, but Oban's splendid situation and its seafront bustle make it a pleasant place. Three miles north, on the A85, is the ruin of Dunstaffnage Castle, the main fortress of the Scots from the 6th century, and a stronghold of the MacDougalls in the 13th century, guarding the great sea-junction of the Sound of Mull, the Firth of Lorne and Loch Linnhe, and with a spectacular inland view to Ben Cruachan (3,695 ft, 1,126m). The visible remains are mainly 15th century. **Dunstaffnage Castle**, *near Oban, Argyll; tel 01631 562465* (open daily, April–Sept, 9.30am–6.30pm).

At Connel Ferry the northbound road to Fort William crosses the Falls of Lora, a geological curiosity formed by a lip of rock at the end of Loch Etive, almost separating it from the sea. The reef is only 6 feet below sea level, while the loch beyond is over 400 feet deep, and at spring tides, there is a considerable waterfall as the tide ebbs and flows across the barrier. Your road remains the A85, following the south side of Loch Etive past Taynuilt, where a side road leads to Bonawe and the remains of 18th-century iron smelting works. The road swings round the foot of Ben Cruachan into the Pass of Brander, a steep defile in which Robert Bruce defeated the army of MacDougall of Lorne in 1308. A long cold finger of Loch Awe reaches into this deep pass; half-way along, you can visit the remarkable Cruachan power station, built deep inside the mountain. **Cruachan Power Station Visitor Centre**, *Falls of Cruachan, Argyll; tel 01866 822618* (open Easter–Nov, daily, 9.30am–5pm).

From here, there is a three-hour climb to the summit of Ben Cruachan. As you approach the main valley of Loch Awe, a prospect of islands is seen, and near the head of the loch stand the impressive ruins of Kilchurn Castle, in a secure island site on Innis Chonell. This keep was the main fort of the Campbells until they removed to Inveraray in the 15th century. The present structure dates from around 1440, and remained in partial use until the 18th century. The Campbell slogan, "It's a far cry to Loch Awe", was indicative of how far their territories stretched.

The A85 leads to Dalmally, from where a minor road branches left, on the line of a former military road, to join the A819 to Inveraray. A mile and a half along, on the left, there is a monument to the Gaelic poet Duncan Bàn MacIntyre

(1724–1812), whose most famous poem celebrates the beauties of Ben Dorain ("mountain of streams") towards which you look, facing up Glen Orchy. From Dalmally, the quickest way back to Glasgow is up the A85 through Glen Lochy towards Tyndrum, where it meets the A82, which you follow to Crianlarich (15 miles); described by one writer as "the most sign-posted nowhere on the planet", it is nevertheless a strategic road and rail junction, at the meeting of three glens and under the peak of Ben More ("big hill"). From here you return on the A82 to Glasgow (50 miles), going down Glen Falloch to traverse the upper end of Loch Lomond as far as Tarbet.

As an alternative, only a little slower and following much less-travelled roads most of the way, continue on the unclassified road beyond Duncan Bàn's monument to join the main A819 for Inveraray (about 15 miles). Here turn left to follow the A83 as far as Cairndow (11 miles), where you turn right on to the A815 and follow the east shore of Loch Fyne, looking across to the miniaturised Inveraray, to Strachur (10 miles). You follow the A815 into the hills and over a low pass to the steep, wooded side of Loch Eck ("loch of the horse" – perhaps a reference to the famous "water kelpie"; see Lochs and Monsters Trail), at the centre of the Argyll Forest Park. This is superb walking country. You are in the district of Cowal, named after an early Celtic chieftain, Comhghall. After Ardbeg (14 miles) you reach the sea again, at the head of Holy Loch.

The A815 follows the shore of the loch, past naval installations, but you can cut off this section by following the A885 after 3 miles to Dunoon (2 miles), which feels a surprisingly large town after the traverse of the empty Cowal landscape. But Glasgow is closer than it seems, and this is commuter country. From Dunoon you leave "Campbell's Kingdom" on a spectacular twenty-minute car-ferry trip across the mouth of the Firth of Clyde to Gourock. Sailing times are frequent (telephone enquiry line 01574 650100; booking line 08705 650000). From Gourock, the A770, then the A8 and M8 lead you directly into Glasgow along the south shore of the Firth of Clyde (25 miles).

TRAIL 19

Viking Scotland: The Orkney Experience

Three days in the Islands

For three hundred years, from the 9th to the 12th centuries, much of northern Scotland, and all the Western Isles, were part of the domain of the Kings of Norway. In 1266 these areas were regained by Scotland. But the northern isles, Orkney and Shetland, conquered from the Picts by King Harold Fairhair in 865, were not regained until 1472, and the imprint of the Vikings remains firmly stamped on them.

To get to Orkney, you can fly from Glasgow, Inverness or Edinburgh to Kirkwall, the island capital. Alternatively, drive up the A9 to the ferry-port of Scrabster (or take the train from Inverness to Thurso). There are regular car-ferry sailings from Scrabster to Stromness on the Orkney mainland (one and a half hours; telephone 01856 850655 for service details). If time allows, the overland route is preferable as it takes you through some splendid landscapes and by fine coastal scenery (it can be partly combined with the Highland Clearances Trail). The short sea-trip also gives a magnificent view of the 1,000-foot sea-cliffs of St John's Head and the 450-foot rock stack known as "The Old Man of Hoy".

Stromness is a sea town, its houses built right out to the water. The name means "headland in the current". Its long narrow main street, so different to that of a mainland town, is a pleasure to walk along, and note the typical Nordic plan of houses set gable-end to the street and fronting on to narrow lanes. It was once a centre of the whaling industry, and a stopping-point for Canada-bound vessels of the Hudson's Bay Company. There were strong connections between Orkney and Canada; numerous Native American women were brought back as brides to the islands. The sea and the maritime heritage are major features of the town's museum; also worth a visit is the Pier Arts Centre, right by the harbour. One of Orkney's great story-tellers, George Mackay Brown, lived here until his death in 1992: his books and poems still breathe life into the landscape and its history.

Stromness Museum, *52 Alfred St, Stromness, Orkney; tel 01856 850025* (open May–Sept, 10am–5pm; Oct–April, Mon–Sat 10.30am–12.30pm, 1.30pm–5.30pm).

Pier Arts Centre, *Stromness, Orkney; tel 01856 850209* (open Tues–Sat 10.30am–5.30pm.) Permanent exhibition of painting and sculpture; also temporary exhibitions.

Day One

Your first trail is of the western mainland. Five miles out of Stromness on the A965 road, signposted to Kirkwall, is a reminder that life on these islands goes back far before the Viking or Pictish eras. Five thousand years ago, while the pyramids of Egypt were new, a race of people lived on this remote archipelago, raised great monolithic stone circles, and built impressive domed tombs. By the Loch of Stenness, turn left on to the B9055; to your left, overlooking the Lochs of Stenness and Harray, are the Stones of Stenness. Park in the lay-by and

Skara Brae Prehistoric Village, Orkney

walk over to the Stones. Wafer-thin and immensely tall, these great monoliths originally numbered twelve, of which three still remain upright, the tallest being over 19 feet above the ground. In the centre of the ring is a stone hearth or platform, probably used for a sacrificial fire. Also signposted from the lay-by is the Barnhouse prehistoric settlement. A few hundred yards' walk will take you to the uncovered remains of 15 huts dating back to the Neolithic (New Stone Age) period, contemporary with the stone circle and perhaps the dwellings of its priests or custodians.

Just over a mile further, where the Ness of Brodgar (the narrow isthmus between the lochs) widens, is the great Ring of Brogar, a circle made up originally of 60 standing stones, of which 27 remain. More than a hundred yards across, this prehistoric monument was in use 5,000 years ago. It is not certain whether it was a replacement for that of Stenness, or used in conjunction with it, but clearly this windswept ridge was a place of great religious significance. Everywhere in Orkney you are aware of the interplay of land and water, but especially here, where the land seems a narrow thread between lakes, sea and sky.

From the Brogar car park, drive back the way you came and turn left on to the A965. In a mile you will see a regularly shaped mound, rising from flat ground, off to the left-hand side. Park at Tormiston Mill, a 19th-century grain mill turned into a "visitor centre", and walk up to Maes Howe. Under the man-made mound, and at the end of a passage 26 feet long and four and a half feet high, is a square-shaped chambered tomb, worthy of comparison with any of the great remains of Greece or the Middle East. Built of great blocks of cut stone, and laid without mortar, it is a testimony to the skill of its builders, who have left no other record of themselves but the silent stones. The chamber was restored in the 19th century, following the break-ins of grave-robbers in the far-off past. In 1153 a group of Vikings explored or sheltered here and left their own graffiti carved in runic letters in the stone: "Ingigerth is the most beautiful of women" says one; "Crusaders broke into this howe" says another – a reminder that the Vikings had sailed to Constantinople (and left runic graffiti in its cathedral of Hagia Sophia as they have here). The small chambers in the walls are believed to have been burial places. At sunset in mid-winter, the setting sun shines directly in through the low entrance passage to light up the inside of the chamber in a way that is clearly part of the building's plan. An interesting website (http://maeshowe.mypage.org/) records "hits" of winter sunshine in the inner chamber.

Maes Howe, *Clouston, Orkney; tel 01856 761606* (open April–Sept, Mon–Sat 9.30am–6.30pm, Sun 2.00pm–6.30pm; Oct–March, as above but closed Thurs afternoon and Fri).

Continue along the A965 for a mile, then turn left on the A986. Orkney place-names are almost all Nordic in origin. The many names ending in -bister show where some Viking settler built his wooden house and established his farmstead during the 10th or 11th centuries; thus Isbister is "Ine's farm", and Swanbister is "Sweyn's farm"; names ending in -setter also indicate a farm, while the many -quoys indicate enclosures of turf or stone for keeping animals. Dounby, 6 miles on, is "dwelling on the hill", and Twatt, 2 miles further, means simply "place", a name related to the many English names that end in -thwaite. (There were many resemblances between Old Norse and Old English.)

Here you join the A967, turning right and following the side of Loch of Boardhouse for two and a half miles. Although notorious for their raids into Scotland, England and Ireland, the Vikings were also farmers, who brought their animals with them and also cultivated grain. The islands have a long tradition of growing oats and barley (Orkney oatcakes are a local speciality) and at the end of the Loch of Boardhouse, one of the old mills has been restored and kept in working order.

Barony Mill, *Springburn, Twatt, Orkney; tel 01856 771276* (open daily April–Sept).

A little further on is the junction with the A966, where you turn left for Birsay. The name means "hunting ground," and here the Norse earls of Orkney had their palace. The ruins here are of a later building, begun in 1574 by a Scottish Earl of Orkney.

Birsay itself is a tidal island, and visitors must watch for the tide or be prepared to be cut off for several hours. If the tide allows, it is an interesting walk across the causeway among rocks and seaweed, but take care not to slip. On the island are the remains of an 11th-century church, a reminder of the Vikings' strange blend of piety and bloodthirstiness. But the first church here was built by the Picts, long before the Norsemen came.

Even if you are not a birdwatcher, you may have noted by now that Orkney is a great place for seabirds. Returning towards Stromness, you branch right on to the B9065 about a mile from Birsay. A mile further, an unclassified road branches right for Marwick Head, a nature reserve where at certain times of the year you can see the engaging puffins, who live in burrows in the cliffs. Here also is the monument to the crew of HMS *Hampshire*, lost in the sea off here in 1916, with the Secretary of State for War, Lord Kitchener, on board.

Another 4 miles on the B9065 takes you to the Bay of Skaill. Park at the Skara Brae car park, and walk the few hundred yards above the beach to the best-preserved prehistoric village in Europe. Dating back 5,000 years to the New Stone Age, the little houses are startling in their neatness and completeness. More than one visitor has felt that the inhabitants had only just gone, leaving their stone furnishings in place. The site is an open one, but it is helpful to visit its informative "visitor centre" and the ticket also entitles you to visit the adjacent 17th-century mansion Skaill House.

Skara Brae Prehistoric Village, *near Stromness, Orkney; tel 01856 841815* (open daily, April–Sept, 9.30am–6pm; Oct–March, Mon–Sat 9.30am–4.30pm, Sun 2.00pm–4.30pm).

For a further view of the Ness of Brodgar monuments, return to Stromness via the B9055 and the A965; otherwise follow the B9056 to where it joins the A967 just before the bridge over an arm of the Loch of Stenness at Voy ("little bay").

DAY TWO

The second Orkney Trail is of the eastern mainland, and the islands linked to it by the "Churchill Barriers". Leave Stromness on the A965 for Kirkwall, and after 2 miles turn right on the A964. This route to the island capital gives you fine views of Hoy ("high island") across the small island of

Graemsay; and as it turns eastward at Houton, it reveals the huge sheltered expanse of Scapa Flow, once the northern anchorage of Britain's Grand Fleet. Here, on 21 June 1919, took place one of the most dramatic – and, to the British, most embarrassing – events in naval history. The German High Seas Fleet, impounded here, was scuttled by its officers. Of its 71 battleships, cruisers and other vessels, only a handful remained afloat. Eleven of them still lie at the bottom.

Just beyond Myre (7 miles) turn right on the unclassified road to Orphir ("reef island"), where between the road and the beach at Orphir bay are the remains of a round church,

St Magnus Cathedral, Kirkwall, Orkney

143

a form associated with the Knights Templar, and built by Earl Haakon of Orkney in the 12th century. Branch left at Orphir village to rejoin the A964 at Cairnton church. Seven miles on is Kirkwall ("Church Bay"). The church is the great Romanesque cathedral of St Magnus, whose steeple dominates the town.

Magnus, the pious earl of Orkney, was murdered in 1115 by his cousin Haakon. The lives and exploits of the Vikings of Orkney are vividly recounted in the *Orkneyinga Saga*, one of the great works of Scandinavian literature. Its narrative of feuds, feasts, lawgivings and epic voyages in the slender wooden longships is highly readable. The cathedral was begun in 1138 by Magnus's nephew, Earl Rognvald. One of its more evocative items is the long double ladder, used by the town's hangman to escort condemned criminals to the top, from which they would be launched into eternity, while the hangman climbed down again.

It was to Kirkwall that the Norwegian King Haakon retreated in 1263 after being repulsed by Alexander, King of Scots, at the Battle of Largs, far to the south in Ayrshire; and he died in the now-ruined Bishops' Palace. Separated from the Bishops' Palace by the 19th-century court buildings, is the quadrangular Earls' Palace, begun in 1606–7 by Patrick Stewart. A member of the royal family himself, albeit via a bastard son of James V, he felt that the king was safely remote in London, and ruled his earldom as a tyrannical petty king. But James VI's arm was long enough to reach to Orkney and have the over-proud earl imprisoned and executed in 1614.

Kirkwall, with its narrow streets and Viking layout, is an interesting town to wander through, with glimpses of the sea at the end of many streets. Tankerness House, by the cathedral, is a museum of Orkney life, charting the habitation of the islands from prehistoric times, through the Pictish, Viking and Scottish eras to the 20th century and the islands' strategic role in two world wars. If you have Orcadian ancestry, the Orkney Room in the Public Library is a useful place to visit.

Kirkwall, St Magnus Cathedral, *Kirkwall, Orkney* (open daily, 9am–5pm; opens on Sundays for services only).

Kirkwall, Bishops' Palace, *Kirkwall, Orkney; tel 01856 871918* (open daily, April–Sept, 9.30am–6.30pm).

Kirkwall, Earls' Palace, details as for Bishops' Palace.

Kirkwall, Tankerness House Museum, *Kirkwall, Orkney; tel 01856 873191* (open all year, Mon–Sat 10.30am–12.30pm, and 1.30pm–5pm, Sun 2pm–5pm).

A 19th-century guide to Orkney announces "no tourist should fail to climb the easy ascent of Wideford Hill", and certainly this 740-foot hill, just west of Kirkwall, is a pleasant walk in good weather and gives a fine view in every direction of the islands and the distant mainland with its mountains. Drive out along the unclassified road branching right from the A964 at the edge of the town, and take the even more minor road to the right after a mile. A quarter of a mile on, the track for Wideford Hill is clearly marked. The walk both ways is done easily within an hour.

Kirkwall has two whisky distilleries, and Highland Park, 200 years old and the most northerly distillery in Scotland, has a visitor centre.

Highland Park Distillery, *Holm Rd, Kirkwall, Orkney; tel 01856 874619* (open for guided tours; charge includes free "dram"; April–Oct, Mon–Fri 10am–4pm; Sat in June–Aug; Nov–March, Mon–Fri tours at 2pm and 3.30pm).

Continuing south on the A961, the road skirts the eastern side of Scapa Flow, running above the cliffs of Gaitnip, near where the battleship HMS *Royal Oak*, torpedoed in a daring U-boat attack in October 1939, still lies as a war grave with her crew. Seven miles on you come to the first of four "Churchill Causeways" built in World War II to prevent further submarine attacks, and now linking the islands of Burray and South Ronaldsay to the mainland. On your left, as the road reaches the islet of Lamb Holm, is the quaint "Italian Chapel", a military hut converted into an ornamental chapel by Italian prisoners of war (usually always open).

About two miles further, on the island of Burray ("fort island"), is the Orkney Fossil Centre, overlooking Echnaloch Bay, which also exhibits a range of antique farm implements. Three miles beyond that you turn right on to the B9043 for the fishing village of St Margaret's Hope, at the north end of South Ronaldsay ("Island of Rognvald", whose brother Sigurd was first Earl of Orkney, around 880). "Hope" means bay. It is here that the little "Maid of Norway" is reputed to have died in

1290, on her way to be crowned as Queen Margaret of Scotland (the bay is not called after her but after St Margaret).

South Ronaldsay has a number of co-operative artistic communities; one of these is here, with several "open studios" (open usually between May and September, though you may find the artists in residence at other times) where you can see artists at work and view (or buy) their products. The old blacksmith's shop is also a museum of "smiddy" work, once vital to a community dependent on horses for land transport (telephone 01856 831567 to check on opening times).

From St Margaret's Hope, retrace the route to Kirkwall, returning from there to Stromness (14 miles) by the A965, over the causeway separating the Peerie ("little") Sea from Kirkwall Bay, and passing the rocky shore of the islanded Bay of Firth. If your time allows, turn right at Finstown (7 miles) on to the A966, and follow this straight road for eight and a half miles, past the little glen of Woodwick, to the unclassified road to the right, signed for "Broch of Gurness". Follow this round the head of the sandy beach to the car park. The broch is on the edge of the sea, looking across Eynhallow Sound towards the low hills of Rousay.

Sometimes known as "Picts' Castles", the brochs are buildings unique to the northern part of Scotland. Built of stone, shaped not unlike the cooling towers of a modern power station, and rising in height to 30 feet or more, they were double-walled towers intended as homes and places of refuge for small communities who lived by the seashore and practised farming and fishing. They were built in the last centuries BC and the first centuries AD; this one is dated from around AD 100, corresponding to the time that Pictish-speaking people are likely to have been arriving in Orkney, where their iron tools and weapons gave them superiority over the bronze-using people already established here.

The Gurness broch is of particular interest as it was partially dismantled by later occupants and the stones used to built the little collection of houses surrounding it. This is the best-preserved Pictish "village" that has been found. Later still, a 9th- or 10th-century Norseman gave the district its present name, Aikerness ("arable point"), and buried his wife or mother along with her brooches in the old broch wall. The foundations of what may have been a Norse hall have also been identified here. There are numerous broch sites in Orkney but this is the best preserved.

Broch of Gurness, *Aikerness, Orkney; tel 01856 751414* (open site).

Returning to the A966, you can follow it round the coast to Birsay, or turn left after a quarter of a mile to cut right across the moors on the B9057 through Dounby, where there is the 19th-century "Click Mill", so-called from the noise of its tall waterwheel, to join the A967 at the north end of the Loch of Harray (turn left for Stromness).

DAY THREE

The third trail takes you to the island of Hoy. There are possible routes from Stromness (passenger ferry) to Moness at the north end, and from Houton on the A964 (car ferry via the oil-terminal island of Flotta in Scapa Flow) to Lyness at the south-east end. Perhaps the best way of doing this trail is to hire bicycles in Stromness and take the Moness ferry out and the Houton ferry back. You will need weatherproof clothes, good walking boots or shoes, and a packed lunch. Hoy has few amenities, which is part of its appeal.

From the Moness jetty take the road to the left, the B9049, for a mile until you reach a junction where an unclassified road, signposted to Rackwick, swings into the interior. Follow this road on the gentle rise up the valley of the Whaness Burn, and after 2 miles you will find a parking area on the right and a marked path (about 15 mins) to the "Dwarfie Stane" on the left. The scenery here is quite imposing, with the cliffs of the Dwarfie Hamars rising above, and a forbidding-looking glen, the Trowie Glen ("trolls' glen") opening up to your right. Dwarfie Stane ("dwarf's stone") is the only known rock-cut megalithic tomb in Britain. Cut out of a single massive sandstone block, it has an entrance with a small burial chamber on each side. As the name suggests, it is hung about with stories of trolls and dwarves, but the real marvel is that such work was done with the Stone-Age implements in use 5,000 years ago.

Follow the Rackwick road round the flanks of Ward Hill, the highest point in Orkney (1,500 feet/479m) to the tiny village of Rackwick (3 miles) at the head of its bay (wick means "bay"). Behind the little schoolhouse rises a 600-foot ridge, to the right of the hill of Moor Fea. Here you leave your car or bicycle. The path to the Old Man of Hoy climbs diagonally up behind the school. Follow it up on to the moors at the top, and a vista of sea opens before you, stretching away towards the Atlantic Ocean.

This whole area is a bird sanctuary, with land birds as well as seabirds. As far as the Old Man, the path is quite well marked, and you arrive at the cliff-top to look across the gap at this great pillar of hard sandstone, with the waves washing across its lava base. Once it had another "leg", joined to the main stack by a natural arch, but this collapsed in the 19th century. It has been climbed several times (a local legend has it that it was first climbed by a lone islander for a bet; when he came down, he found he had left his pipe at the top, so he went up again). Apart from the obvious hazards, one climber encountered the habits of the fulmar petrel, which practises projectile vomiting as a weapon against intruders, "leaving a pungent odour on skin and clothing which no amount of scrubbing or deodorant can remove".

By walking along the cliff top to the right for 2 miles, it is possible to reach the top of the mighty cliffs of St John's Head, which fall 1,000 feet sheer to the sea, but the way is rough, boggy and treacherous. The walk to the Old Man should take between 50 minutes and an hour, each way. Look out for the wide-winged skuas, or "bonxies" as they are known locally. They nest on the high moors above the sea, and can act threateningly to walkers who stray from the path.

From Rackwick to Lyness is an 8-mile cycle ride, with some ups and downs, but not too strenuous, back to the B9049 and turning right, a quiet road that offers fine views out past the islands of Cava, Fara and Flotta to Scapa Flow. Lyness has a museum in its old naval base, explaining the role of Orkney in the two world wars.

The Hoy Trail has a sense of adventure about it and will leave lasting memories of a unique landscape.

Recommended Reading: *An Orkney Tapestry* by George Mackay Brown

TRAIL 20

The Trail of Bonnie Prince Charlie

Four days, from Inverness to Lothian, Skye and back again – the Rising that captured Edinburgh and struck terror into the Londoners – but failed to restore the Stewart dynasty.

In 1688, King James II of England and VII of Scotland was forced to give up his throne and flee to France; his place was taken by his son-in-law William of Orange and his daughter Mary. After William's death, James's younger daughter, Anne, became queen. During her reign England and Scotland became the "United Kingdom", in 1707. Many people hoped or expected that on Anne's death, the son of James VII and II would be called from exile to inherit the throne. But the exiled Stewarts were Catholics and this was unacceptable to the Protestant majority.

On Anne's death in 1714, the throne went to the German prince George of Hanover, a very distant connection of the Stewarts, but a stalwart Protestant. James's descendants, living in exile in Europe, were out in the cold. But many people, especially in Scotland, wanted to see the restoration of the Stewarts to their "rightful" throne. In 1689, 1715 and 1719 there were armed risings in Scotland, aimed at defeating the Hanoverians. Supporters of King George called the Stewarts "Pretenders" to the throne; and the Stewart loyalists were known as "Jacobites", after the Latin form of James, Jacobus.

Although the Stewarts remained a Catholic family, religion was only one of the issues: many Scots backed them because of hostility to the Union with England. Jacobitism was particularly strong in the Highlands, and it was said that 30,000 armed men could be raised there to fight for the cause. Encouraged by such thoughts, Prince Charles Edward Stewart, grandson of James VII, decided on his own in 1745 to go to Scotland and raise the clans on behalf of his father, "The Old Pretender". After meeting initial reluctance, he raised an army, had early success, and invaded England. There things went sour. Only 150 miles from London, his advisers forced him to turn back. So began the long retreat that ended in the Battle of

Blair Castle, Blair Atholl, Perthshire

Culloden, in April 1746 – and the final extinction of the Stewart Cause.

The trail starts from Inverness (links here with the Monster Trail). In fact you follow the route of the Monster Trail down the Great Glen on the A82 as far as Fort William (67 miles, see pages 66–71). From Fort William take the A830 westwards, signed for Mallaig, and follow it for 30 miles. This road swoops and swings through rugged and beautiful country; about 2 miles after passing Beasdale Station, park by the Prince's Cairn above Loch nan Uamh ("Loch of the Caves"). The modern cairn marks the spot where the adventure began and ended.

On 25 July 1745, a French ship, the *Du Teillay*, dropped anchor off here, on the shore of South Morar. On board was Prince Charles Edward Stewart, and he came ashore at Borradale. The local clan chiefs, despite their traditional Stewart allegiance, were far from pleased to see him. He had brought only seven men, no arms, and very little money.

From here in August 1746, at the end of the adventure, a courageous French captain took the fugitive prince and a few followers to safety in France.

The trail now turns back along the A830. If your time allows, turn right at Lochailort (6 miles) and follow the A861 southwards through splendid scenery for 13 miles to Kinlochmoidart. In a meadow here stands a row of seven beech trees to commemorate the "seven men of Moidart" who landed with the prince. Return then to the A830 following the route along which Charles proceeded eastwards to Glenfinnan (14 miles), at the head of Loch Shiel. Though some of the leading chiefs ignored him, over a thousand clansmen rallied to his call. The royal standard of the Stewarts was raised here on 19 August, and James VIII and III was proclaimed King of Scotland, England and Ireland.

The memorial tower here was built in 1815 by Alexander Macdonald of Glenaladale. The figure on top is not Prince Charles Edward, but an anonymous Highlander. The statue was added in 1834 to mark the heroism of the prince's followers. There is a vistor centre on the other side of the road. Here the Glenfinnan Highland Gathering takes place every August.

Glenfinnan Monument, Glenfinnan, Inverness-shire; tel 01397 722250 (open April–May and Sept–Oct, daily, 10am–5pm; June–Aug, 9.30am–6pm).

Eighteen miles to the east, in Fort William, the West Highland Museum has an interesting collection of Jacobite relics, including an "anamorphic" portrait of the prince, which looks almost meaningless until viewed on a polished metal cylinder, when the prince's likeness is immediately apparent. The fort here – of which almost nothing remains – pre-dates the '45; it was set up under King William II in 1690, to control the warlike and pro-Jacobite clans of the region.

West Highland Museum, *Cameron Square, Fort William, Inverness-shire; tel 01397 702169* (open all year, Mon–Sat 9am–5pm; July–Aug, also Sun 2pm–5pm).

Fort William and the area immediately round about have numerous other non-Jacobite visitor attractions. The trail takes you on to the house of Achnacarry, to the side of the great Glen, 5 miles north of Fort William, still the seat of Cameron of Lochiel, whose ancestor was visited by the prince. At first unwilling to "come out", Lochiel was finally persuaded by the prince, and was with him to the end of the campaign, being one of those rescued and taken to France in the following year. Achnacarry House is not open, but a museum in its grounds is dedicated to Clan Cameron's history and worldwide ramifications. **Clan Cameron Museum**, Achnacarry, near Fort William, Inverness-shire; (open Easter–mid Oct, daily, 1.30pm–5pm; July–Aug, 11am–5pm).

The Jacobite army marched east and then south, ironically, over military roads that had been built to speed up the passage of government troops across the Highlands. Return from Achnacarry to Spean Bridge (7 miles) where the A86 branches off to the right from the A82, and follow the A86 up through rocky Glen Spean, past Loch Laggan ("loch of the hollow") to Laggan (29 miles). Bear right on the A889 for Dalwhinnie (9 miles); just after this high-up village you rejoin the main A9 north–south route through the mountains at Trinafour. Sleeping rough and living on oatmeal bannocks, the Highlanders followed this way through the bleak Pass of Drumochter and down to Blair Castle at Blair Atholl (24 miles).

Turn left on to the B8079, which makes a loop through the village, first passing the Clan Donnachie (Robertson) centre and the opportunity of a scenic half-hour's walk up the Bruar River to the Falls of Bruar. At Blair the white-walled castle, bright against the green hills, home of the Duke of Atholl, played host to the prince both on his way south and in retreat. Its armoury and other rooms are open to visitors, and here too are many memorabilia of the Jacobite rebellions. In 1745 the ducal family of Murray was deeply divided. The duke supported the Hanoverian government, while his two brothers supported the Stewarts. One of them, Lord George Murray, was the prince's chief general.

There is a local museum in the old school in the main street of Blair Atholl village.

Blair Castle, *Blair Atholl, Perthshire; tel 01796 481207* (open daily, April–Oct, 10am–6pm).

Blair Atholl Museum, *The Old School, Blair Atholl, Perthshire; tel 01796 481232* (open July–Sept, Mon–Fri 10am–5pm, Sat–Sun 1.30pm–5pm).

Continue south on the A9, passing high above the **Pass of Killiecrankie** (9 miles; see Rob Roy Trail). The Highlanders threaded through the pass where, 56 years earlier, their grandfathers had routed the forces of William of Orange in the very first Jacobite rising. Take a loop off the A9 to enter the little cathedral town of **Dunkeld** (17 miles) where a handsome stone bridge built by Thomas Telford in 1809 spans the River Tay. The cathedral was already mostly a ruin in 1745, lead from the roof having been used to make bullets in the Battle of Dunkeld, in the first Jacobite Rising in 1689; but the choir has been restored as the parish church, and the little houses of the cathedral close are most attractive. One of Scotland's finest 16th-century poets, Gavin Douglas, was a bishop here; when he was appointed he had to fight his way in against a rival faction.

From here rejoin the A9 for the last 15 miles to **Perth**. This town was quickly occupied. So far, hardly a shot had been fired, and Edinburgh lay open to the Highland army. The government force, under Sir John Cope, had been outmanoeuvred. It had gone north to meet them, by the wrong route.

In Perth, the prince was able to regroup and assess his strength, and plan the next moves. The trail takes us to Edinburgh (40 miles), following the M90 motorway from Perth. Some of the Prince's men followed this route, commandeering boats to cross the Firth of Forth at Queensferry where the two great bridges now span the gap, though most took the land route via Stirling. By 17 September 1745, they were in the fields outside Edinburgh, below the Salisbury Crags to the east of the city. The city, still walled, had shut its gates, hoping that Cope and his men would get back in time to save the day. But when the Jacobites promised not to loot, the gates were opened, the few guards fled, and the city surrendered. The prince installed himself in the ancestral palace of Holyroodhouse, and gave receptions in what would nowadays be called a "charm offensive" on the apprehensive civic dignitaries. Only the castle remained still loyal to King George, but its small garrison could not influence events. Equally, the Jacobites could not storm its massive walls. In any case, they had a fight on their hands elsewhere.

The government army was ferried over the Firth of Forth and formed itself up at Prestonpans, a salt-panning har-

"The Five Sisters of Kintail", Wester Ross

bour town 3 miles east of Edinburgh. Prince Charles and his men went out to face it, and on the morning of 21 September they routed the redcoats with a single Highland charge.

For Prestonpans, leave Edinburgh on the A1, signed for Berwick, and turn off left for Cockenzie and Port Seton (10 miles). The site of the battle is marked by a cairn, just by the junction with the A198. It must be said that the presence of power lines, a railway track and the giant Cockenzie electricity generating plant do nothing to preserve the atmosphere of that day, when a single, devastating Highland charge routed the redcoat troops. General Cope fled to Berwick, soon pursued by a sarcastic Scottish song: "Hey, Johnnie Cope, are ye walking yet?"

Charles returned in triumph to Edinburgh and his court at **Holyrood Palace**. But apart from some Highland reinforcements, few joined his army. Leaving Edinburgh on 31 October, they marched across the Southern Uplands. Part of the army, following the route of the present A73 and M74 roads, crossed into Clydesdale, over the summit at Beattock, and down into Annandale. Another contingent marched south towards Kelso on the Tweed, then turned south-west from there, up Teviotdale and through the narrow valleys that once were the homes of the dreaded Border Reivers, Eskdale and Liddesdale, before joining up with the others on the Solway Moss. Ten days after leaving Edinburgh they crossed the Border into England.

But on 20 December they were back, fording the River Esk at Longtown, heading north again. They had come within 150 miles of London before the prince's advisers had persuaded him that they did not have the resources to capture the English capital. The people of England had not rallied to the Stewart cause, and armies were being raised to oppose the invasion. The prince was angry and despondent. The longed-for triumph had seemed so close. But there was still hope. The Highland army was setting about the siege of Stirling when news came that a government army under General "Hangman" Hawley was on its way. They moved south to intercept it, and at Falkirk they won their last victory, on 17 January 1746, just to the south-east of the town.

The trail resumes at **Falkirk**. Leave Edinburgh by the M8, signed for Glasgow, and at Junction 2 (4 miles) turn on to the M9, signed for Stirling. Follow this road to Junction 5 (12 miles), where you take the A803 for Falkirk (3 miles). After passing Callendar Park on the left, turn left on to the B8028, and follow it for just over a mile, then turn right on to the B803, just by Falkirk High railway station. In half a mile, take the minor road to the right, signed for Greenbank. This road skirts the battlefield site and brings you to the monument, just off the road on the right-hand side, about a mile along.

A monument marks the battlefield site at Greenbank. Industrialisation here, as at Prestonpans, has utterly changed the appearance of the place. Charles Edward stayed at Bannockburn House, the site of Scotland's most famous battle being only a few miles away. General Hawley was taking tea in Callendar House, 2 miles in the other direction, when he was informed that the Jacobites were attacking, and rushed to the scene. As dark came on, and in pouring rain, the Highlanders withstood a cavalry charge and then hurled themselves on the infantry, who turned and fled.

Despite this victory, the retreat northwards continued, the army retracing its steps through the wintry mountains. By 18 February, they had reached **Inverness**, and many clansmen returned to their homes in the glens. The citadel was captured by the Jacobites, and the prince established himself for seven weeks in a house in what is now Church Street.

The trail returns to Inverness from Edinburgh, via the M8, M90 and A9 roads (158 miles). As the A9 passes Dalwhinnie (about 50 miles north of Perth), you glimpse the silver sheen of Loch Ericht over to the left. Far down this long narrow loch, on the slopes of Ben Alder, the prince spent some time hiding in "Cluny's Cage" – the mountain hideout of the chief of Clan MacPherson – a location vividly described in Robert Louis Stevenson's *Kidnapped*.

This is Macpherson country; the clan's museum is in Newtonmore, 12 miles north of Dalwhinnie (on a signed loop off the A9 on to the A86), as is the larger part of the Highland Folk Museum, with reconstructed buildings and interiors showing the life of Highland people through the centuries. It is a useful reminder that for many people, in the '45, life went on as usual. There might have been a war, but crops had still to be planted and harvested, to maintain their near-subsistence life-style.

Highland Folk Museum, *Newtonmore, Inverness-shire; tel 01540 661307* (open April–Aug, Mon–Sat 10.30am–5.30pm, Sun 10.30am–5.30pm; Sept–Oct, Mon–Fri 11am–4.30pm).

Kingussie is less than 3 miles north of Newtonmore on the A86 or A9; if on the A9, follow signs to the A86 into the village, on the left. The Highland Folk Museum is in Duke Street, off High Street on the east side, with artefacts and displays that recreate the life of ordinary people in this part of the Highlands in past times.

Highland Folk Museum, *Kingussie, Inverness-shire; tel 01540 661307* (open April–Aug, Mon–Sat 10.30am–5.30pm, Sun 1pm–5pm; Sept–Oct, Mon–Fri 10.30am–4.30pm: guided tours only).

The trail leaves the main road here for a short detour to Ruthven Barracks (1 mile east of the village, on the B970: open site). This imposing structure, set on an artificial mound, was part of the London government's dispositions for policing the Highlands. It was fired by the Jacobites in 1745. It was here, too, that the shattered elements of the prince's army came to regroup after Culloden.

The library and museum in the Highland capital have much Jacobite material, though the town itself has grown and altered enormously. The citadel near the harbour, built by Cromwell's forces in the 17th century, has vanished. The castle is a 19th-century construction, on the site of the original fortress. In front of it stands a statue of Flora Macdonald.

Inverness Museum & Art Gallery, *Castle Wynd, Inverness; tel 01463 237114* (open all year, Mon–Sat 9am–5pm; July–Aug, also Sun 2pm–5pm).

Slowly, a government army under the Duke of Cumberland, younger son of George II and, at 25, the same age as Prince Charles Edward, plodded up after them. A depleted Jacobite army was assembled for the inevitable battle. Cumberland's force was at Nairn. The Jacobites tried, and failed, to mount a night attack on 15 April 1746. The prince's weary men were forced up on to Drumossie Moor, 5 miles to the east of Inverness. Charles had spent the night at Culloden House, now a hotel. At that time it was the home of Duncan Forbes of

Culloden, the man who, more than anyone, had persuaded the Highland clans not to support the rising. On 16 April the two armies met in the last great battle fought upon British soil. The Hanoverian artillery and musketry defeated the Highlanders. In less than an hour, the battle was lost. The prince was led from the field, reputedly in tears.

It was the end of the campaign. For five months the prince was on the run in the Highlands and Islands.

The battlefield, by the B9006 road, is in the care of the National Trust for Scotland, and has been restored to something like its appearance in 1746. It is possible to stand there in the wind and the heather and relive the grim morning of 16 April, 1746. There is the Memorial Cairn of 1801, and numerous stones mark the "Graves of the Clans" and other features like the "Well of the Dead" where dead clansmen were thrown. The Cumberland Stone is said to be where Cumberland – whose brutality after the battle earned him the undying hatred of the Highlanders and the name of "Butcher" – studied the lie of the land before the battle. It was not a Scotland–England battle, but a Jacobite–Hanoverian one; many Scots fought in the duke's army. The site is open, but there is an "interpretive centre".

Culloden Moor Visitor Centre, near Inverness; tel 01463 790607 (open all year, daily, 9.30am–5.30pm; July–Aug, 9am–6.30pm).

The prince, with a few followers, fled westwards, and sailed from Loch nan Uamh for Benbecula in the Outer Hebrides. Remaining nowhere for very long, since government soldiers and spies were everywhere, he travelled north into Lewis and south again to South Uist. It was here on 28 June that Flora Macdonald (whose father was a Hanoverian officer) dressed him as her maid "Betty Burke", and set out "over the sea to Skye", fooling the government militiamen.

The Prince's Trail now takes you to the west coast again, this time west from Inverness in a great arc through the wild and mountainous country in which he took refuge. Leave the town on the A82, signed for Fort William, and follow it down the side of **Loch Ness** as far as Invermoriston (26 miles) from where you head west on the A887, travelling through rugged, forested country to Bunloinn (16 miles) to join the

A87, signed for Kyle of Lochalsh (41 miles). Past Loch Cluanie, impressive mountain ranges rise up on each side. As the road drops into Glen Shiel, below the fine mountain group known as the "Five Sisters of Kintail", you pass on the right the site of the Battle of Glenshiel, scene of an earlier Jacobite defeat in the short Rising of 1719. Followers of the Rob Roy Trail may like to know that the veteran swordsman fought at this battle. Just below the bridge over the River Shiel, a footbridge carries the track to the battle site. The crag above, Coire nan Spainteach, is a reminder that a detachment of Spanish troops fought with the Jacobites.

From Kyle of Lochalsh a new bridge (toll to pay) links Skye to the mainland. At Kyleakin, just on the other side, is the Bright Water Visitor Centre, with exhibits on local ecology and history. Follow the A87 for 34 miles to Portree. The room where the prince and Flora said goodbye is now part of the Royal Hotel in Portree, the main town of Skye. Flora Macdonald was put on trial, imprisoned for a year, emigrated to North America but returned, and her grave can be seen at Kilmuir on the Trotternish Peninsula (23 miles north of Portree; follow the A87 to Uig, then the single-track A855). It quotes the comment of Dr Samuel Johnson, who met Flora on his famous visit to the Western Isles: "Her name will be mentioned in history, and if courage and fidelity be virtues, mentioned with honour." There is a museum of island life at Kilmuir, also a "heritage centre" introducing the long history of Skye, located just as you enter Portree from the south.

Skye Museum of Island Life, *Kilmuir, Trotternish, Isle of Skye; tel 01470 552213* (open Easter–Oct, Mon–Sat 9.30am–5.30pm).

Aros Heritage Centre, *Portree, Isle of Skye; tel 01478 613649* (open May–Oct, daily, 9am–9pm; Nov–April, Mon–Sat 10am–6pm).

The prince returned to the mainland at Mallaig, and lived rough until 19 September 1746, when the French vessel *L'Heureux* picked him up and bore him away to a lengthy exile in Rome. Although he is said to have made one or two incognito visits to London, he never saw Scotland again.

Recommended Reading: *Culloden* by John Prebble

TRAIL 21

Empty Glens: The Sutherland Clearance Trail

Two days, from Inverness

Notes:
1. If you plan to stay overnight in the vicinity of Bettyhill, it is advisable to book ahead, as accommodation is limited.
2. Much of the driving in Sutherland is on single-track roads with passing-places. These should be used to allow cars to overtake as well as for cars passing in opposite directions.

If you have done the Rob Roy Trail, then the sight of long, desolate glens, with traces of fields and houses still visible on the hillsides, will be quite familiar to you. This trail explores two areas where the reasons for this desolation are revealed.

Many factors lie behind the forced eviction of large numbers of people from the Highlands and Islands in the course of the late 18th and the 19th centuries. The chief ones were economic and social. In many places, ownership of the land was still in the hands of clan chiefs. Once upon a time their prestige had depended on the number of men they could muster. After 1745, they were incorporated into the British aristocratic structure and their prestige depended on wealth. Much clan land was sold to new landlords whose sole interest was in getting as large an income from it as possible. The introduction of large-scale sheep farming required the good valley land, where the people grew their crops, as well as the less productive hillsides; and sheep farming required very few workers.

The Highland people lived in small communities called clachans, groups of thatched stone houses. To the eye of the southerner, these seemed squalid and primitive dwellings. One shocked American compared them to the huts of African tribesmen. The people spoke Gaelic and still wore tartan. Many spoke no English. Their diet was principally potatoes and oatmeal. To the landowners, and the factors (land-agents) employed by the landowners, they were a survival from the past, almost another species. There was no understanding of the Highlanders' way of life; they were simply an obstacle to "progress", to the full economic exploitation of the land.

The Highlanders themselves lived there because they always had. They paid rent, in cash or kind, but they felt, in a deep-seated sense, that the land was theirs. Emigration had always been part of their experience; large and hardy families were born in these "black houses" and many went south or abroad when they grew up. But many stayed. In 1800, more than a third of the Scottish population lived in the Highlands (today, less than a tenth).

To the more desperate and ruthless landowners, even people could be a crop. Youngsters were sold into the American slave trade in the 18th century; proprietors received government bounties for the soldiers and sailors they could supply to fight in the Napoleonic Wars. When the landowners wanted to clear whole villages and districts, they called in police and troops to back up their own strong-arm squads, who moved in, emptied the houses of what they had, and set them on fire. The law was on their side; usually they were the law, as local magistrates.

From Inverness, the trail leads northwards on the A9, across the Black Isle. At the junction with the B9176 (about 24 miles) turn left and follow this "scenic route" signed to Bonar Bridge. After 2 miles, you leave the green coastal lowlands behind and climb into the heathery moors. Around the lonely Aultnamain Inn (8 miles), peat is cut for the numerous whisky distilleries of the region. Four miles beyond the inn, you come in sight of the Dornoch Firth, and one of the great views of Scotland opens up, best seen from the outlook point at Struie Hill, where the mountains of Sutherland and Wester Ross are spread before you. An indicator in the car park points out the peaks. By the shore of the firth (2 miles), you join the A836, turning left for Bonar Bridge, but at Ardgay (4 miles), turn left on to the minor road for Gledfield and Strathcarron. A narrow road runs along each side of the River Carron here; you are on the south side. Both sides of the river were well-populated in the early 19th century.

At Greenyards (6 miles), also spelt Gruinards, is the scene of a violent confrontation on 31 March 1854. A strong detachment of 35 police and sheriff's officers had come here in order to enforce eviction orders on the villagers (there was a population of some 300 people here). It was the women who formed the front ranks of the protesters; they refused to back off, and the police charged in. There was a furious battle, with sticks and stones against cudgels and swords, which left many of the demonstrators severely mauled and injured. The incident became known as the "Massacre of the Rosses", though perhaps only one of the women was actually killed.

Continue up Glen Carron and after about 3 miles turn right to cross the river, then left to Croick (3 miles). At the little church here is one of the few physical traces left by the evicted clansfolk. Nine years before the Greenyards clearance, the same landlord had turned out the people who lived in Glen Calvie, a now utterly unpopulated glen which joins Glen Carron just across the river here. About 500 people were forced out; 90 or so, with nowhere to go, camped in the churchyard, and scratched messages in the church's east window which can still be seen. With poignant Calvinistic fatalism, they blamed

View of Dornoch Firth

themselves for their fate: "Glencalvie people the wicked generation" says one of these messages; another says "Glencalvie people was in the Churchyard here May 24 1845". A special correspondent of the London *Times* witnessed the evictions and their consequence. A copy of his angry but reasoned account is displayed on a notice-board in the church.

Return to Ardgay (about 12 miles), and turn left on to the A836, signed to Bonar Bridge, and follow it over the bridge that crosses the Kyle of Sutherland. In the 19th century, the county and the dukedom of Sutherland were almost one and the same thing; the duke owned almost all of it. As you come up to the railway viaduct at Invershin, look across to Culrain on the other side. In spring 1820 there were riots here when a community of 600 people was forcibly evicted. As they had nowhere to go, they said they would as soon die on the spot as anywhere else. Women were again in the forefront, but it did not stop the military from attacking them with bayonets. Follow the A836 through Lairg (11 miles) and on through the empty landscape, under the peaks of Ben Klibreck to Altnaharra (21 miles). The inn here was rebuilt with the timbers of the parish church of Farr; the church was pulled down because there were no people left for it to serve. A mile past Altnaharra, turn right on to the B873, on the north bank of Loch Naver, and follow the narrow, twisting road into the green valley of Strathnaver towards Syre (about 17 miles). Approaching Syre through the Naver Forest, look out for signs for Rossal.

In this area, woods were planted in the 20th century over the site of the crofts of the evicted villagers. The trees have now been cleared from the clachan of Rossal and signs have been put up to explain the remains that can still be seen. From recently found archaeological exploration it has become clear that this area had been inhabited since the New Stone Age – several thousand years of continuous human settlement that were brought to a sudden end in 1820. By the roadside is a monument to Donald Macleod, who was born here, witnessed the brutality of the clearance, and wrote a book to expose the human disaster behind the "improvement" of Sutherland by its ducal owners. He describes how he climbed the slope behind the village to see 250 houses on fire all the way down the strath. At that time around 1,900 people lived in Strathnaver.

From Rossal continue to Bettyhill (about 15 miles). This coastal township is named after Elizabeth, countess and duchess of Sutherland; it was built to house a few families evicted from Strathnaver, a cosmetic exercise of no value to the vast majority of the cleared population. The Strathnaver Museum, on the A836 at the east end of the village, tells the story of the area. There is also a Clan Mackay Room, as this is the ancient territory of the Mackays.

Strathnaver Museum, *Bettyhill, Sutherland; tel 01641 521418* (open April–Oct, Mon–Sat 10am–1pm, 2pm–5pm).

From Bettyhill, go east on the A836, along the top of the Scottish mainland with views north-west to the Orkneys (only the northern-based Vikings could have called this area Sutherland, "southland") for 18 miles to the junction with the A897, 2 miles beyond Melvich. A short branch off to any of the tiny coastal settlements, like Kirtomy or Portskerra, will reveal what sort of coastline the ousted crofters were supposed to make a living on: the wave-lashed cliffs and rocky coves are scenic, but no place to start a fishing industry with sailing boats.

The A897 runs inland, up the long Strath Halladale, across the watershed and into the Strath of Kildonan. The rivers here are famous salmon streams.

From the road you may well see herds of deer moving on the hillside. The landscape is not as scenic here as it is further west; great tracts of Sutherland are more like the tundra country of Lapland than anywhere else. But here too, a large population once lived. They were forced out in 1819. Hugh Miller (see Beginnings of Geology Trail) wrote:

> …*the victory of the lord of the soil over the children of the soil was complete. In little more than nine years a population of fifteen thousand individuals were removed from the interior of Sutherland to its sea-coasts or had emigrated to America. The inland districts were coverted into deserts through which the traveller may take a long day's journey, amid ruins that still beat the scathe of fire, and grassy patches betraying, when the evening sun casts aslant its long deep shadows, the half-effaced lines of the plough.*

Kintail mountains, Wester Ross

That desert remains.

Yet the desert produced gold. At Suisgill (30 miles), on the left-hand side, is the location known in Gaelic as Baile an Or, "place of gold", where the discovery of gold in the stream led to a small-scale gold-rush in the 1880s, when hundreds of people came to prospect. Details of this period and of other significant times from the prehistoric era are in the Timespan Centre in Helmsdale (10 miles on from Suisgill). This fishing village is overlooked by a ruined 15th-century castle which was the scene of Borgia-style poisonings in the 1560s.

Timespan Heritage Centre, *Helmsdale, Sutherland; tel 01431 821327* (open April–June and Sept–Oct, Mon–Sat 9.30am–5pm, Sun 2pm–5pm; July–Aug, Mon–Sat 9.30am–6pm, Sun 2pm–6pm).

At Helmsdale, if your time allows, turn left on to the A9 and follow it for 4 miles as it rises over the hill barrier of the Ord

of Caithness. Look out for a sign to Badbea, off to the right. From the parking space, follow the path down to this clifftop site. On this slope, pitched at such a degree above the sea-cliffs that young children were tethered to prevent them falling, a small community, resettled from the interior, lived for a few years and struggled to keep alive. The sites of the houses are still apparent, and a small monument records the wholesale departure of the people for New Zealand. The area is now utterly deserted. A short walk along the cliff top – care needs to be taken, especially on windy days – takes you to the inner end of an airy geo, or sea-canyon, where seagulls fly below you and seals haul up on the stony beach at the foot of the cliffs.

From here the Clearance Trail returns south, beside or close to the sea all the way, via the A9 to Inverness (about 70 miles), though there is also a possible northward link to the Viking Trail at Scrabster Pier, via the A9 to Latheron and Thurso (45 miles).

INDEX OF PLACES

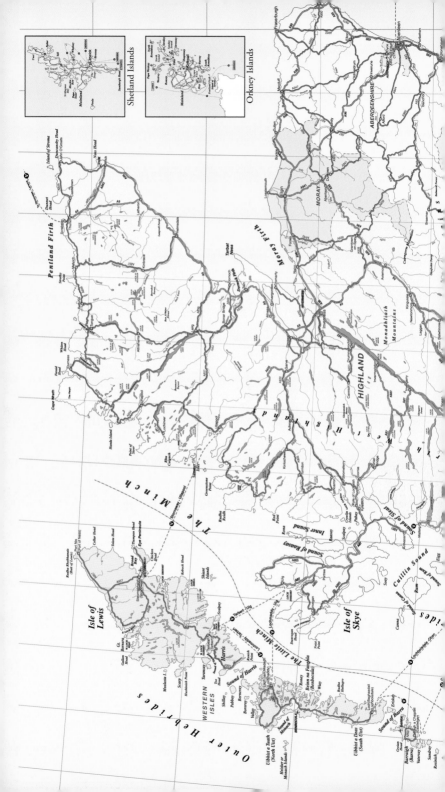